Mel Gibson

by

JOHN HANRAHAN

LITTLE HILLS PRESS

Cover: Sygma

PHOTO CREDITS.

P.4. Childers/Sygma, P.6 Childers/Sygma. P.8 Mitchell Library P.11 News
Ltd., P.12 LHPress, P.13 LHPress. P.14 LHPress. P.17 Sygma, P.18 (Top)
Associated/V.Roadshow, LHPress, Avalon, P.21 V.Roadshow, P.24 Avalon,
P.25 Avalon, P.27 Hoyts/Universal City, P.28,29,30 Hoyts/Universal City,
P.32.33. 35, V.Roadshow/K-M, 38 Pisces, P.39 Michael Pate, P.40 (top)
Michael Pate (bottom) Adrian McKibbons. P.43 Associated/V.Roadshow, P.44
News Ltd. P.45 Associated/V.Roadshow P.47 V.Roadshow/K-M, P.48
McElroy/CEL, P.49,50-51,52 (top) Hoyts/de Laurentis, P.52 (bottom)
McElroy/CEL, P.55 CEL, P.57 News Ltd, P.60 Hoyts/de Laurentis, P.64
Hoyts/MGM-UA. P.66 V.Roadshow/Warner Bros., P.69 V.Roadshow/Warner
Bros., P.70,71,72, Hoyts/MGM-UA, P.75 Fabian/Sygma, P.77 News Ltd, P.79
Associated/V. Roadshow, P.81 Pisces.

First published in 1986 by
Little Hills Press Pty. Ltd.,
P.O. Box 60, St. Peters. 2044 N.S.W. Australia

© Dojiw Pty. Ltd.

Typeset by Deblaere Typesetting Pty. Ltd.
Printed in Hong Kong by Colorcraft Ltd.

ISBN 0 949 773 34 4

ACKNOWLEDGEMENTS

My thanks to Phil Avalon, Charles Burfitt, Wendy Day, Dale Evans, Allan Finney, Paul Fischer, Jackie Kent, Lisa Keogh, H.G. Kippax, Paul Lindenschmid, Br. Patrick Lynch, Jim McElroy, Mark McGinnity, Adrienne McKibbons, Aubrey Nellor, Michael Pate, Di Rolle, Pam Saunderson, Dean Semler, Bill Shanahan, Babette Smith, Margaret Smith, David Stratton's *The Last New Wave,* The Australian Film Revival, Angus and Robertson, 1980, Alex Ying, the publicity departments of Village Roadshow, Hoyts, CEL and EMI/THORN, and St. Leo's College, Wahroonga.

A special thanks has to go to my family for enduring me during this project.

CONTENTS

INTRODUCTION

MEL Gibson is the face and, for many, the body of the 1980s. His success has been phenomenal, his appeal vast, from teenage girls to tough bikies, from middle-class yuppies to maiden aunts.

Why? What has he got that the next guy doesn't have?

The story of his rise, in less than a decade, the movies he's already made and the people with whom he has worked and spent time is amazing. For example, would he be where he is today if one of his family hadn't arranged a drama class audition and then a former drama student mate had been less keen to get him a role in a small surfing road movie? Would he have won the role in a movie called *Mad Max* if he hadn't come to the audition bearing the bruises of a fight at a party?

Just what is it about this Aussie movie heart-throb and sex symbol that has made him, in the space of five years, one of the most sought after and highest-paid stars in the world?

Much of it is the mystery that surrounds his successful efforts to keep his private life very much to himself and his family. Where there is mystery there is inevitably curiosity and, while Mel has been generous and open (sometimes by his own admission too open) in dealing with the press, he retains a private world far from the so-called glamour of Hollywood. Home for him, his wife Robyn and their four children is a six-bedroom house in the Sydney beachside suburb of Coogee and a farm in the southern Australian state of Victoria.

He has found, as have other internationally successful Australian actors, directors and music industry performers (Bryan Brown, Fred Schepisi, Peter Weir, Gill Armstrong, the Little River Band) that it's just as easy, far more comfortable and far less nerve-wracking to live in Australia than anywhere else. The rest of the world, after all, is just a phone call and a plane flight away.

Australia, he has insisted, is the place he calls home. And that's

Eva Mylott, Mel Gibson's grandmother

despite the fact that he still retains American citizenship, having
been born in Peekshill, New York state, on 3 January 1956. He
migrated to Australia with his parents and 10 brothers and
sisters in 1968. His heritage runs deep on both sides of the Pacific
and he is careful to keep everyone happy. After saying in
America that, despite all the cynicism, he was proud of American
citizenship, Australians demanded to know if he still loved them.
He told me twice, during the shooting of *The Bounty* and after
finishing it, *The River* and *Mrs Soffel* that Australia was his
favourite country in the world. 'It's not that I don't love
Australia and Australians. I do. I married one, I've fathered
(then) three! My grandmother was Australian. I have a home
here!'

Mel's media-hyped status as a so-called sex symbol contrasted
with reactions to his casual appearance in public.

When he returned to Australia in 1984 an established star and
certainly a household name and agreed to do interviews for his
latest film to be released, he lay sprawled on the grass of a small
open park area near Sydney's Circular Quay ferry terminal.

It was an overcast winter's day and Mel, sporting a thickish
stubble of a beard and wearing a warm coat, plucked at random
shoots of greenery. He had been lying there for almost an hour
chatting about the trio of films he had completed in the past
fifteen months ... *The Bounty,* on locations in the South Pacific
and London, *The River* in Tennessee and *Mrs Soffel* in a wintry
Canada.

Just after lunch, around 2.15 pm, we had strolled the 200
metres from the foyer of the Regent Hotel to the park area.

Along the brief walk, perhaps 30 or 40 people passed us. Not
one took a second glance. For the entire hour we spent lying in
the middle of the park Mel remained completely at ease as
dozens of people strolled past just 20 metres away from one of
the world's hottest movie stars.

It remains one of the amusing enigmas of Mel Gibson that
quite often he is not instantly recognised in real life. The star of
nine films, the face that has now appeared on countless magazine
covers around the world, a photographer and cinematographer's dream, somehow disappears into the crowd. He's
even managed at times to elude the attention of airline staff,
politely and unintentionally, when boarding planes.

Understandably, that inexplicable level of anonymity is something he cherishes and has no intention of changing. But, like so
many before him, he is a victim of his own success. Whether he
likes it or not, he is, to a very large degree, public property. Like
hundreds of movie stars before him he has found his way into the
hearts and minds of millions around the world. For that he must
pay a price that, most people would agree, is high, but has com-
pensations.

But there is much over which he has no control. In February 1985, the American magazine *People* featured him on the front cover, describing him as 'the sexiest man alive', the face of the decade, the man most women would want to go to dinner or bed with. I asked him how he felt about the sex symbol tag, one of the great media cliches.

'I'm too old to be a sex symbol,' he retorted with a gentle, almost self-mocking laugh. 'I'm getting beyond that now. I'm not young enough to be one anymore. Who's taken in by that sex symbol stuff any more, anyway? Give it to somebody else, I'm interested in pursuing something else now.'

That's not how tens of millions of fans who flocked to see *Mad Max Beyond Thunderdome* around the world see him. In virtually every country of the world he ranks in the top ten favourite movie stars.

In France in 1985, *Beyond Thunderdome* opened to record box office for a non-French film.

Mel has achieved extraordinary success in Japan, purely because of the *Mad Max* trilogy.

Alex Ying, managing director of the films' distributors, Warners Bros. in Japan, explains 'All of his other films, including the ones that achieved wide international acclaim and some box office success, like *Gallipoli* and *The Year of Living Dangerously*, have failed to take off here. But the *Mad Max* films are such huge successes that everyone here identifies Mel with the character. Normally, sequels do only about 70 per cent of the previous film's business, but *Thunderdome* has been a huge hit.

'He is among the top 10 international stars here in Japan. He would probably be ahead of Redford and Newman.

'His appeal is highest among young men and women, with a 70 per cent skew in favour of men. It is mainly as a macho hero that they like him, although older women like him as a sex symbol. But the kids really squeal if they see him coming down the street and they recognise him.'

Ying says the lone, solitary figure of Mad Max against the evil forces and tremendous odds appeals to the young Japanese. 'Almost like the figure of the Samurai who would roam around the countryside by himself getting ambushed all over the place but coming out destroying the bad guys in the end.'

The innately polite Japanese, it seems, let their hair down when Mel comes to town, as he has done for each of the *Mad Max* films. 'They even follow him into restaurants to get his autograph, and I think he has some very strong fans among the female press here.'

THE GIBSON FAMILY

THE Gibson family connection with Australia goes back to 1862 when Mel's great-grandfather, Patrick Mylott, arrived from County Mayo in Ireland.

In 1867, he claimed portions of land on the edge of Lake Tuross on the far south coast of New South Wales. Patrick had been a farmer, wine and spirit merchant and shipowner.

Nine years after his arrival, Mel's grandmother, Eva Mylott, was born. Her life and career played a major role in changing the course of at least part of the family's history for, by the turn of the century, she had become one of Australia's foremost opera singers.

So fine was her voice that she became a protegée of the great Dame Nellie Melba, who arranged for her to go to Paris to study with Madame Marchesi. In February 1902, Eva Mylott gave a magnificent farewell concert at the Sydney Town Hall before her departure on a British tour.

In January 1907 she left for the United States, where she performed in Boston, Montreal and Philadelphia. Newspaper reports of the time described her as a 'small, titian-haired singer' and her voice, which developed from soprano to contralto, was widely praised.

On 17 June 1914 in Flushing, New York state, she married Hutton Gibson, a partner in Gibson Bros. Brass Founders of Chicago. The marriage took place at the Church of the Blessed Sacrament, and she moved to live with her husband in Montclair, New Jersey. Eva Gibson never forgot her family, her home town or her country. She wrote regularly to Australian friends and, during World War I, she donated medical instruments to Australian hospitals.

In October 1918, Mel's father, John Hutton Mylott Gibson, was born; followed fifteen months later by his uncle, Alexander Mylott Gibson.

Eva died tragically less than a month after Alexander's birth, at the age of forty-four. She had asked to be buried at Mt Olivet, Chicago.

Both her sons, Hutton and Alex, were to arrive in Australia as part of their war service during World War II. They landed in Melbourne and had hoped to visit the home of their late mother, but a call for active duty prevented that.

Hutton Gibson and his family did not return to Australia for another twenty years; in 1968 after being injured in the US, where he had worked for a rail company, Hutton settled for good and started a new life with his young family.

They settled at Mt Kuring-gai on the northern outskirts of Sydney where, among other things, Mr Gibson pursued a highly successful career as a quiz show contestant.

To date, three members of the family – Mel, his older sister Sheila and his younger brother Donal – have pursued careers in the entertainment industry. Sheila worked as a singer, Donal as an actor in Sydney.

Mr Gibson later moved his family to Brisbane, where he now lives with his wife Anne.

SCHOOLDAYS

Ha, Ha What have we here? Mel in his only school production, 1968

Ha! Ha! What have we here?

AFTER Mel arrived in Australia with his parents in 1968, he and his brothers attended St Leo's Christian Brothers School in Wahroonga, a northern Sydney suburb. Mel was twelve when he arrived at St Leo's, with a strong American accent. He travelled to the school with his brothers from the family's home a few kilometres further north.

Before long, he acquired the nickname 'Mad Mel', after a popular radio personality in Sydney at the time. After leaving St Leo's, he and his brothers transferred to the nearby Asquith Boys High School.

Mark McGinnity, now a schoolteacher in Sydney, recalls Mel at St Leo's. 'The thing that impressed me most in those early times was his high-spiritedness. He used to enjoy provoking teachers quite a bit.

'He was crazy. We had a maths teacher, quite an eccentric character who used to hit us with a strap if we did silly things. Three of us had a competition to see who could be strapped most often in a day; Mel won it easily. He was strapped about twenty-seven times. Now you see him on interviews and he always seems so reserved and quiet.

'He used to mimic teachers, too, and make up dirty ditties about them. Anything to provoke them.

'He was a fairly well built young guy, but his younger twin brothers were better footballers than he was.' Mel seems to have done better at athletics. 'I think he was a reasonable runner, but he was better at the field events because he was so strongly built,' Mark added. 'He calmed down a bit as he got older and became a lot quieter in his manner.'

For those who think of Mel with the familiar close-cropped, rugged haircut, it is surprising to learn that, in Mark's words, 'He grew long hair, of course. It was right down on his shoulders.'

Mark recalled that because of Mel's strong American accent, he was given a hard time by some of the students. 'He took it fairly well,' Mark added.

As far as he could remember, Mel did only one piece of acting at the school, in a melodrama when he was about fourteen, as part of a schools competition. 'He was the baddy, and he hammed it up really well, wearing the black cape and carrying away the damsel,' said Mark.

'We had an elderly drama teacher, a really tall skinny lady whom we called Sticks Russell. I saw Mel after he'd done *Tim;* he said he was making movies, and added, "Ah, if Sticks Russell could see me now!"'

St Leo's had Shakespeare oratory competitions but, as far as Mark could recall, Mel never entered any of them. 'I don't recall him ever declaring any great passion for acting or any other specific career as he got older,' Mark added. 'He seemed to be a very average guy, in every way.'

Brother Patrick Lynch taught Mel at St Leo's. 'He was not particularly remarkable or outstanding. I was surprised when I found out later on that he was acting,' he added.

He always had a larrikin quality. I've gone to see him in his films and I've seen him in some of his stage roles. In his films, I look at him and think, 'Yes, that's Mel all right. I can't see what everybody's excited about. That's just what he was like.

'And I know from talking to him a little since he became successful that he was more interested in acting than being in film, but he was making money out of his films. When he was doing

St. Leo's College, 2nd Form, 1968

his early *Mad Max* films, he made sure he continued his theatre work.'

While Brother Patrick admires Mel's concern and love for the stage, he admits to being less than happy with another aspect of Mel's professional life. 'I get quite irritated by him in interviews, because it's not Mel Gibson talking,' he says.

'It's as though he doesn't want to be there, to acknowledge that he's a public figure. I look at him and think that's not Mel Gibson, he's more than that. He was always an easy-to-talk-to sort of guy, but when I went to talk to him after seeing him in *No Names, No Pack Drill,* he almost didn't want to know me. He was nervous and embarrassed.

'I called around to see him after *Death Of A Salesman;* I thought he was superb in that. I waited until he settled down and relaxed. We just passed the time and he talked about his wife and kids. He was quite relaxed. But that's what strikes me about him on the screen ... he is himself. He's not pretending to be someone else.'

Basketball – so much for cricket!
Under 14 team

BUDDING ACTOR

IT may seem impossible to imagine, but Mel Gibson never intended to become an actor. He didn't even make the first move that would lead to his extraordinarily successful career in such a relatively short space of time. Credit for that goes to one of his sisters who sent in, unknown to Mel, an application form for an audition with the National Institute of Dramatic Art in Sydney.

'When she told me that she had done it, I didn't really go for it much, but then I sat down and said, "Well, why not? Why not two days out of my life?" But I felt I was going to make a jerk out of myself in front of a lot of people,' he told Margaret Smith for *Cinema Papers* magazine in March 1983.

But he did not. He passed the audition and was accepted for the acting course at NIDA.

'My earliest memory of him was that he had long hair. He was with students who were doing all the work but was quite shy and retiring,' recalls Aubrey Mellor, one of Mel's drama tutors.

'He used to tell stories about his family and obviously had immense pride in his parents, particularly his Dad. He was a good and warm person. He gave all the appearance of coming from a warm and loving home.

'He never called attention to himself early on. Towards the end of the first year, we finally became a bit annoyed with the long hair and said, "Tie it back, here's a rubber band, pull it back!"'

The difference was significant. 'You actually saw that he had a mobile face; everything that was happening inside him could be seen on his face.

'When you saw his face, you realised that anything he thought would be revealed on it. It showed that he had a future in films.

'He has always moved well, so he had no physical problems, and he has a good voice with no vocal problems. His singing voice is a very pleasant baritone.

'In the second year Mel was there; I taught comedy classes he took. Mel is outstanding. He's one of only two actors I know in this country who is a genuine slapstick artist. He can do the whole pratfall thing... walking into walls, falling flat on his face. Most extraordinary. In class comedy work he was way ahead of the others. Some would do more character work, but he would really do good physical comedy; Three Stooges and the Marx Brothers sort of stuff. He was able to screw his face around and do Donald Duck and all those things.

'And he's a very good character actor, by which I mean he tended to build up the effect of a totally different person by altering his voice, attitudes to the world, some physical characteristics and emerging as a different person. To me, that's not the best acting. It's clever acting, but really good acting, the most honest, involves the actor transforming himself from the inside. The character actor is really hiding. Basically, Mel felt secure in being someone else; he could be quite bold. He is still basically shy although he obviously has much more courage in his acting now.

'Halfway through that second year I remember a tutorial with him and saying, "You have a certain look, and when you leave here, people are going to grab you and use you for leading male roles... You are actually going to get those parts, and you should do them!" But he wasn't particularly keen on doing them because he never saw himself as the romantic lead.

'I then cast him as Romeo in a production by the Sydney director Richard Wherrett with Judy Davis as Juliet.

'He didn't argue about it, but he was never a troublesome student and he's a very trusting person. He's been lucky because people haven't misused him in the industry. He's much shrewder than he was; in his younger days he could have been misused if anyone had wanted to. In this case he simply said he'd have a go at it. Mind you, I don't think he had many preconceptions about it... I don't think he was particularly well informed about great classical literature, so he wasn't overawed by it.

'He might have thought Romeo was a bit of a milksoppy role, but he made it his own. He brought a wonderful boyish quality to it that was quite outstanding. Of course, people later knew about it and John Bell had heard Mel's reputation and cast him in the professional production.'

Mellor found it interesting that Mel stuck with the acting course. 'He was always one of the boys, but he could have left at any time. At that age it's easy to drift into something else if you don't find something interesting. But he was always there, he did the exercises, putting in the work.'

It was really in his second year that Mel's star qualities began to emerge. Mellor again: 'I directed him in *Mother and Son*, an early Australian play by Louis Esson, in which he was the lead.

Mel Gibson with wife, Robyn and daughter Hannah on the set of *The Bounty*

Gallipoli – Mel Gibson as Frank

Robbie (Phil Avalon) and Scollop (Mel) in *Summer City*

Judy Davis played a widow from the shanty town, Steve Bisley was the son of the squatter up the road, and the play had a wonderful scene where the two men gamble for her. They were very good. Mel's was a very straight role, in which he had to call up a lot of himself… and he was very good.

'Then he was in *The Hostage* as a dumb Irishman, a member of the IRA, I think, a military man… with one ear pushed forward. He was very, very funny. For his graduation piece, he had one of the leads in *Once In A Lifetime,* the Kaufmann and Hart play about vaudevilleans in Hollywood at the invention of the talkies. Mel played a dumb American.'

One of the best insights into Mel's acting career and his more experienced attitudes to the media coverage of him emerged in an excellent interview by film journalist Paul Fischer. At the time of the interview in January 1983, Mel had made two *Mad Max* movies and five other films including *Gallipoli* and *The Year of Living Dangerously.* He had also done nine stage plays, including *Romeo and Juliet, No Names, No Pack Drill* and *Death Of A Salesman.* Fischer asked Mel whether his acting aspirations stemmed from his earlier American childhood or his experience since arriving in Australia, in 1968. 'The latter,' said Mel, 'I think probably the fact that I'm a hybrid who spent half my time in America and half of it over here helped; I found it took a little acting in youth to settle into the new environment of Australia.

Rebel (Mel) Cathy (Noni Hazelhurst) in *No Names, No Pack Drills,* Opera House, 1980

'Acting wasn't really something I had a burning desire to do.

'I fell into it quite by accident, I suppose. I did an audition [at NIDA] because at the time I had a few choices and I thought: What's the point of not doing something? I got accepted so I snatched the opportunity.

'I remember the first time I appeared on stage. I couldn't remember the lines and a curious thing happened to my knees, they wouldn't support me and I had the shakes.'

He recalled feeling extremely nervous, wanting to fall down in those early days. 'It halved itself each time I went on stage. The next time I was able to stand up and concentrate and remember and the lines would come. Now it's just a matter of butterflies before opening night.

'Stage is a very important training ground. It doesn't teach you specific film acting techniques. It just solidifies the whole basis of acting for you. But I don't prefer either. I just prefer good roles.'

Paul asked him for a retrospective assessment of his earliest film roles. 'When you look back at something like your first film role, it's as if you had no part in it. After a lapse of four years you look at it and you can't remember what you did, or why, or what you were thinking at the time. You just look at somebody with your outer shell doing it. But you can use that as a kind of measuring stick for your own development.

'And you can see mistakes, glaring mistakes, that you didn't detect at the time, which is good. I'm glad when I see things like that.'

Fisher also invited him to comment on his attitude to the media, ever-watchful since stardom has been thrust upon Mel, and whether, at times, the coverage about him made him angry. 'Angry? Well, there have been times when I wanted to cheerfully strangle someone. When something comes out, you think, "My God! I didn't say it!" It's so easy to misinterpret or twist, but I couldn't care less now. If I do an interview and leave it with someone, then it's my own fault. It doesn't bother me now.

'I think the public are smarter. The reason I was angry at first was because I thought people would read it and believe it.
'But most people are smart enough not to believe what they read to the letter. And I also thought, who reads it anyway?'

Was he, Fisher asked, surprised or awed by his own success?

'No, I'm not surprised. I could smell it coming... you see, there are good and bad things about being successful.

'It's good because you get a lot more work; the negative side is that there are certain expectations, which really goes against what you're trying to do, if you're trying to find your way into a role or character who's different. It's difficult to be totally believable when there are expectations involved [for the audience], when they just don't go and see some guy for the first time. You have to try twice as hard. Although you get the opportunities, it is still harder to make them work.'

The choice of roles, he admits, comes down very much to instinct, particularly with characters he doesn't like to play.

'I look at a script and I've got a good nose about what I don't want to do. I can't even get into specifics. I just have to look at it and I say, "nah". It may be something I don't believe in.'

Mel admitted to Margaret Smith of *Cinema Papers* that he has always enjoyed entertaining people from an early age. 'I used to get a kick out of affecting people, no matter what sort of effect. That is what drives you on,' he added.

Acting, he said, also creates the dream to hide behind. 'When you have a mask on, you can do almost anything... pull your pants down in public, whatever. It doesn't matter if you have a bag over your head.'

The one actor that recurs in Mel's comments about acting in some way is Humphrey Bogart. Not surprisingly, there were others who perhaps subconsciously caught his eye along the way, as he told Margaret Smith in the *Cinema Papers* interview.

'I used to look very closely at guys like Spencer Tracy and Clark Gable. Tracy had a modern acting style, twenty or thirty years ahead of what Gable did. He was still doing that wooden, 1930s stuff, but he had an appeal that just used to shine out of him. I take little pieces from everywhere. It is "pass the ball", isn't it?'

His observations now have a certain irony about them, because when it comes to assessments and comparisons of Mel with the spectrum of stars through film history, his style, his roles, even his looks, recall some of the greats from the so-called golden years of Hollywood. He has been the clean-cut conservative hero, often fighting for a principle, with a good woman by his side, a journalist, soldier, a Navy man, farmer, a sympathetic prisoner.

Even among the mayhem of the *Mad Max* trilogy, Max remained the steadying influence, the man whose simple heroics would eventually save the day.

For someone who is regarded as a sex symbol, Mel Gibson is not a macho hero in his movies. A passionate staircase kiss with Sigourney Weaver in *The Year of Living Dangerously*, a kitchen sink embrace and kiss in *The River*, tender moments through the jail bars in *Mrs Soffel*; these have been characteristic.

Bedroom scenes? Well, yes, there have been a few, brief and gentle, with unambiguous dialogue and hardly enough of anything to be described as 'seductive' by the most imaginative film publicist. There have been no naked bedroom romps; at least figuratively, one foot has always been on the floor.

But for millions of women around the world, that's all that's necessary. They love his eyes, an engaging smile that can suddenly break into a larrikin grin and a cocky walk. They're the physical attributes that embody that mercurial, perhaps intangible, quality of 'charisma'.

Whatever that is, Mel Gibson has it in abundance.

As Dean Semler, the Australian cinematographer who photographed both *The Road Warrior (Mad Max II)* and *Mad Max Beyond Thunderdome,* said: 'He looks a million dollars through the lens. You don't want to take your eye off him... He has classic good looks. It wouldn't matter what he was doing. He just oozes charisma. An enormous presence, a strength. Judy Davis has it, Bill Holden had it.

'And it doesn't matter what kind of lighting you use for Mel... you could play him under flouros, clouds. He's very good to light. Good, hard sidelight works well on him. And he's good at it. He doesn't have to do a thing. He just stands there. I'm saying he's working very hard to do nothing... he might move one eyebrow a quarter or an eighth of an inch and it's enormous on the screen. He knows how to make his face work. The slightest movement will move mountains.

'He's a good specimen all round. I can't fault him anywhere.'

One of the most consistent things to emerge in talking to people who have worked with or known Mel over the years, from the time he first arrived in Australia, is that the personality of that same high-spirited, sometimes cheeky, youngster who endured being called 'Yank' in disparaging tones has basically not changed.

He bears no chip on his shoulder, is generally immaculately polite and likable to the point where people who have had only fleeting contact with him feel in some way protective.

But that is not to say he has been, or is, an angel. There are plenty of tales about him kicking up his heels, drinking and partying into the early hours of the morning.

As producer Jim McElroy observes: 'I don't think the fact that he lives life to the fullest is bad at all. I think that it shows in his acting... in his worldly experience, in his eyes and his face on the screen. And you know where I think the qualities we're seeing in his acting on screen come from? This may sound high-faultin' sort of language, but I think it's an inner security out of faith and family. And that's developing more and more. And I believe, I sense in him, a degree of faith, whether it's religious or self faith and a great family strength, both from the family he came from and his own family now. That allows for the late nights and the drinking parties and the hard work and the separations and a deep trust.'

SUMMER CITY

MEL'S first film was a small-budget (Aus$150,0000 road movie called *Summer City*, set against the spectacular surfing beaches on the east coast of Australia. While it has become forgotten in his growing list of important credits, it played a significant part in his getting one of the key roles of his career.

There are several versions of how Mel was given his first movie break. At the time, in 1975, he was still a student at the National Institute of Dramatic Art. A Sydney actor, screenwriter and sometime model, Phil Avalon, was producing and co-starring in the film, which he'd also written. He'd raised the money by grabbing virtually any modelling job he could get and buying and selling second-hand cars.

'I'd buy the cars at auction on Tuesday for $200 or $300, take them home and with an electric polisher brighten them up and paint the tyres. Then I'd advertise them for $800 in the weekend paper,' Avalon recounts.

'I'd cast John Jarratt, by then a young NIDA graduate who'd had a few roles including one in *Picnic At Hanging Rock,* and was looking for a couple of more young actors.

'It wasn't me, as I've been credited, who discovered Mel at a NIDA graduation, but Johnny. Mel hadn't even graduated when John suggested I have a look at him. He knew the characters in the script and felt Mel might be right for one of them.

'He arranged for me to pop along to see a rehearsal of something the students at NIDA were doing, but I couldn't get to it. I was too busy, but John was pretty keen to get Mel onto the picture and brought him around to my house.

'He rolled up and was perfect for the character of Scollop... quiet, shy and inarticulate,' Phil said.

'It wasn't a big role. He was really just part of the furniture on

Mel as Scollop, in *Summer City*

that film and a fall guy for Steve Bisley's character Boo. He was a sounding board.

'I must admit I didn't think he was very good-looking then... very Aussie-boy-next-door-looking... so he was perfect. I cast him on the spot. He didn't even read.'

At that stage, Mel had little idea of the direction in which his career might go.

Summer City was not even being made for conventional theatrical distribution. 'I was shooting it on 16-millimetre for the surf movie circuit, so it was just a low budget effort,' Phil added. Mel got a whopping $400 for the role.

'We were pretty broke and I'd financed the whole film. I had overdrafts everywhere. The $20,000 I had in my pocket was for the film stock and camera, and a bit of food for the boys to go up to the location,' Avalon recalled.

'Steve [Bisley] and Mel turned up at my house one evening on NIDA holidays and said they wanted to go up to get a feel of the location. This was around November 1976.

'So the two of them got into the old Chevy that was the star of the show. It was during a petrol strike. They had to milk the tank of a car that had crashed over a cliff near my place to get enough petrol to drive up to the location.'

The pair of young actors, armed with sleeping bags, slept in an old Returned Servicemen's League hall that also became production office, hotel and interior sets for the film. The rest of the cast and crew followed a week later.

Added Avalon: 'They slept on the floor. There were three or four rooms, one for wardrobe, and there was a bar and games

24

room for everyone, but most of them slept on the floor next to the stage. It was unbelievable when you think back.'

One of the sequences in the film required Mel to ride a surfboard, so he and Steve spent the week up there attempting to master the basic points of board riding. In vain, as it turned out. 'We had to get a stand-in to do the scenes,' Phil added.

Shooting the film was, for most of the people concerned, more an adventure than anything else. The cast and crew put in long hard days, starting early in the morning. But at day's end, they were ready to play and, not surprisingly, they did.

'Well, Bisley is a lovely bloke, an outstanding actor. But he was a rogue. And Steve and Mel were bloody close mates,' said Phil.

'They did a lot of things together. One of the girls in the cast, Debbie Forman, was madly in love with Mel.'

Inevitably, some of the lads got up to the kind of pranks any nineteen- and twenty-year-olds are likely to.

'The hall was booked for a wedding reception one Saturday night and we had to get out of the building until around midnight,' recalled Avalon.

'I was paying $100 a week for this hall. We weren't too happy about having to move and we were shooting seven days a week. And everyone had either gone to the pub or gone out with their girls.

'When we got back, we suddenly found ourselves surrounded by angry locals who started to let our tyres down and were trying to get me out of the car to bash my head in. They were bashing

John Jarratt, Phil Avalon, Mel and Steve Bisley in *Summer City*

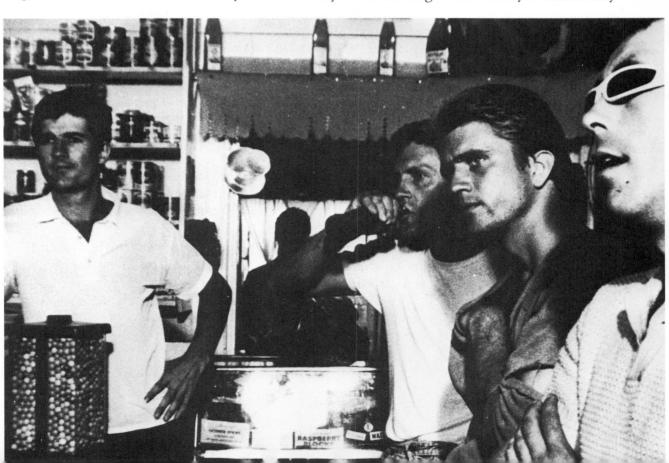

on the window and everything, trying to get at me.

'What had happened was that Steve and Mel had been outside the hall when all the guests came out... with their trousers down and their backsides exposed. Obviously the locals didn't take too kindly to that kind of mucking around!'

While spirits generally remained high, Avalon's funds did not. He was struggling to meet most of his payments on the film, including those to his band of young stars. Unfortunately, there was a falling out between Avalon and his cast.

'It was over money. I simply didn't have any... and at the time John Jarratt's father, who appears briefly in the film, was managing them,' recalled Avalon.

'He was a wonderful bloke, but he and I would clash a lot as John was doing a play at the Sydney Opera House, almost 100 kilometres south, and would drive down every night and drive back to the location in the morning. And I'd get him to drop off film at the laboratory. His old man would say, "Well, how about slipping him an extra $10 for the gas" and I just didn't have it. In the end, we just fell out, me and the actors. It was right at the end. And when I look back, they were right, too. I was pushing them pretty hard. But we just didn't have the dough.'

When the shoot was finally over and everyone had returned to Sydney, John, Mel and Steve offered to do Avalon a favour; to pick up the surfboards used in the film from the coastal location and bring them back to Sydney.

To 'fund' their gesture, Avalon told them to take a stack of empty Coca-Cola bottlers left over from the shoot.

'So they loaded them up, took them back to the location and cashed them all in to buy the petrol and get the car back for me,' explained Avalon. Months later, while Mel completed his NIDA course and was finally cast in *Mad Max*, Avalon managed to get a theatrical release after getting the print blown up to 35 mm. He and partner Austin Levy launched and promoted the film around Australia. It was eventually released through the Greater Union organisation and opened in December 1977 at the old Century Theatre in Sydney.

Critics were less than thrilled by it and, it seemed, failed to notice Mel in his supporting role as Scollop, but by that stage it didn't matter. Mel Gibson's career had already taken its most significant steps forward.

While *Summer City* flickered on the soon-to-be-closed Century cinema screen, the twenty-one-year-old was starting work on *Mad Max 1*.

Mel Gibson as Tom Garvey in *The River*

The River. Tom (Mel Gibson) and
wife (Sissy Spacek) contemplate the
devastation of the flood

Scene from *'The River'* Sissy Spacek
and Mel Gibson

MAD MAX I

IF there was one single springboard to stardom for Mel Gibson it was his casting in the title role of the original *Mad Max*. But at that point, right at the start of his professional career, no one foresaw the stardom that would burgeon ahead of him in less than a decade.

Sydney casting director Mitch Matthews remembers testing Mel for the role. 'He was one of about a dozen young actors we called in and tested for the part,' she recalled.

'I remember he came along late one night, after rehearsals for the final-year production at the National Institute of Dramatic Art. He was, understandably, a little tired, naturally shy but very, very polite. We recorded his test, a scene from the film, on black and white video. Unfortunately, I don't have it any more, but I remember that Judy Davis and Steve Bisley both came along that night. While we tested Steve for a role I think George Miller also did a test with Judy, simply because she was there.

'Mel was basically no different from any other actor until, of course, you saw him on screen. He did the test very well. I think I preferred the way he did the test to the way he eventually did the role in the film.

'And as I was looking through the camera I was thinking, "Oh, brother, wow! What is this we've got here? The old shivers down the spine!' We looked at the tape and said, "It's just got to be him, he's fantastic".'

Ironically, the film was almost never made after being knocked back by a key production company in Melbourne where George Miller and his friend and fellow-producer Byron Kennedy lived.

Alan Finney, the national marketing and advertising director of the Village Roadshow Corporation, one of Australia's major distribution and exhibition chains, was involved in a dual role. He was a director of Hexagon Films, partly owned by Village

Roadshow, to whom Miller and Kennedy originally brought their idea. 'When George and Byron bought a thematic outline, not a script, to us at Hexagon which was then a production arm of Roadshow partly owned by us and director Tim Burstall, we thought, to be honest, that the stunts could not be done in Australia,' admits Finney today.

'I plead, now, utter stupidity. But reading the outline, we just said no one in the country could do the stunts they were proposing, and certainly not on the budget they were proposing.

'Then John Lamond, who is now a producer in his own right, set up a meeting with Roadshow's managing director Grahame Bourke. Graham, being the visionary that he is, just fell in love with George and Byron. He just said, "I trust these two men to produce the film they say they will produce".

'One of the things George and Byron wanted to do was avoid casting any known face... anywhere... in *Mad Max*,' Finney recalls.

'The one person they did cast who might have been known was Roger Ward... but they shaved his head so that he'd be unrecognisable, because what they deliberately set out to do was not to have anyone in the film who brought with them, him or her, any connotation from television.

'They wanted to impose such a unique and individual vision on the film they didn't want any carryover associations.

'Mel at that stage was a totally unknown quantity. His face had never been seen and George's instincts about him were absolutely correct.'

Mad Max

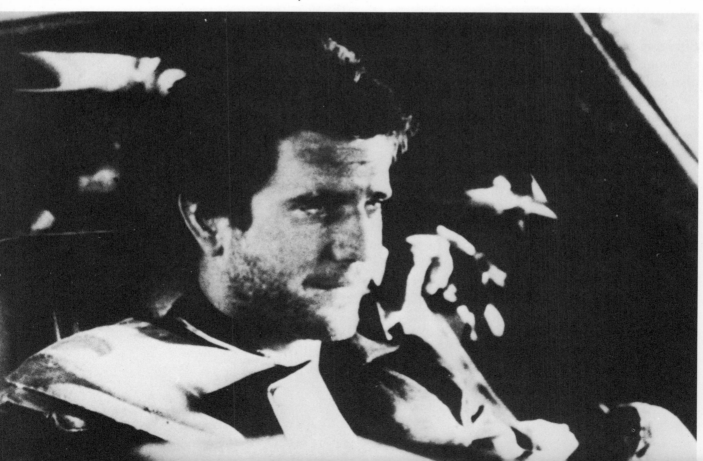

Mel's unexpected graduation 'gift' after NIDA was something that any aspiring and ambitious young actor could only dream about, but not even the most optimistic actor could have imagined what it would lead to. Indeed, Mad Max I would forever change the course of Mel's life, launching him, literally, to international stardom.

At the end of October 1977, his comprehensive course at NIDA finished and, like all the other graduates, he wondered when or if he would find professional paying jobs. But, unlike some of his peers, he didn't have to wait, because he was immediately cast in Mad Max I, the small-budget ($400,000) but highly ambitious futuristic road movie to be shot in Melbourne. His close mate and fellow NIDA graduate Steve Bisley was also cast in the film, as a fellow highway cop. Neither could have guessed what lay ahead of him.

Mel in *Mad Max* with Steve Bisley

Mad Max had been conceived by Dr George Miller and his close friend and associate Byron Kennedy. Miller, who came originally from the small Queensland town of Chinchilla, had been making short films for some seven years.

A twin, he had moved with his family to Sydney where, after completing secondary education at Sydney Boys' High School, he graduated from the University of New South Wales medical school and took up residency at St Vincent's hospital in Sydney.

But his irresistible passion was movies, and in 1971 he attended a vacation film school in Melbourne, where he met Byron Kennedy, himself a keen short film maker. The pair collaborated on a number of short films, most notably *Violence In The Cinema Part 1,* a satire on cinema violence featuring actor Arthur Dignam flatly delivering a learned lecture on film violence as all manner of things are done to his body. It won two Australian Film Institute Awards and was screened at a number of festivals around the world.

Miller worked as a locum to fund his film-making ambitions and among the screenplays he developed was the story of a young pursuit cop who ends up battling a gang of outlaw bikers.

The screenplay had caught the eye of Village Roadshow, one of Australia's three major distribution and exhibition chains, which agreed to underwrite the film for a distribution guarantee.

Kennedy and Miller's concept (the screenplay was co-written by Miller with journalist James McCausland) set the film somewhere in the not too distant future where, as he described at the time, 'urban society is in terminal decay. The inner city highways have become white line nightmares. The arena for a strange, apocalyptic death game between nomad bikers and a handful of young cops in souped-up pursuit cars.'

Much about the story was distinctly original, down to the comic-book style of character names (Toecutter, Jim Goose, Johnny The Boy, Silver Tongue and The People's Observer).

Roadshow's commitment to the film only followed Kennedy and Miller's successful efforts to raise money from the private sector and independently complete the shooting of the film, but more of that later.

Before Mel arrived in Melbourne for the shoot, Miller and Kennedy had already run into an unpredictable disaster. Rosie Bailey, the actress originally cast as Max's wife, came off the back of a motorbike riding to the film's location outside Melbourne. She and the driver, stuntman Grant Page, broke their legs. Production was halted for two weeks and Joanne Samuel was signed from the Aussie TV series *The Young Doctors.*

Mel later recalled to me his rather chilling introduction to the film... before he even got onto the set. He'd arrived at the flat he was due to share while shooting the film.

'The door opened and I was greeted by a guy with bandages,' he explained.

'It was Grant Page, the stunt co-ordinator on the picture, who'd also busted his nose as well as his leg. It seemed everybody was in a state of despair.' Such physical disasters were to become fairly familiar sight around the sets of all three *Mad Max* films as the stunt men pushed themselves to their limits to come up with more and more breathtaking, eye-popping crashes, rolls and chases for George Miller's cameramen.

Mel did some of the less dangerous driving as his character, Max Rockatansky, set out to revenge the cold-blooded murder of his son, Sprog, his terribly injured wife Jessie, and the death of his police force colleague Jim Goose, played by Steve Bisley.

Of course, Miller and McCausland had created the framework for a highly sympathetic character among the high-speed mayhem and suggestive violence. Mel fleshed out the character perfectly, taking him from a frustrated but diligent cop with a wife who begs him to quit to a brooding, determined hero confronting almost impossible odds and, of course, ultimately overcoming them.

It was, in many ways, classic stuff, the creation of a new version of the road movie genre. But Mel's achievement was all the more notable for being able to match and stand out against the carefully orchestrated pace and spectacle of Miller's direction.

Mel later acknowledged that he liked the pace of the film, and observed, 'It's a director's film – the storyline, editing and music all contribute so much. You have bad guys and not so bad guys.

A tender moment amidst the mayhem of *Mad Max*. Max (Mel Gibson) with his wife Jessie (Joanne Samuel)

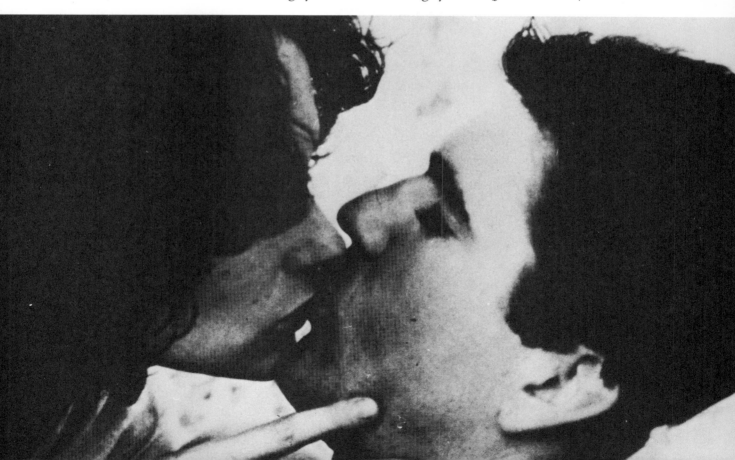

'There are not really any goodies, just some people you can really sympathise with. It's like a western on wheels.'

And that, quite astutely, summed up what the film was all about.

Four years later, after *Mad Max II,* when he was able to see the film and the character in greater perspective, Mel told Margaret Smith in an interview for Australia's *Cinema Papers* (March, 1983): 'Oh, that was fun, because you have your cardboard guy there. The story is comic book style and everyone is ready to laugh at it. The images are cartoonic, so to slot into that mould, you have to slip into that style. You can't do something totally different; it just doesn't work. Then you have the problem of the character being a closet human being. He has to interact with other characters and yet not appear to. It is a little tricky.'

The Australian critics, the first to see it without the inhibitions of preconceptions, were generally positive about the film, with a few notable exceptions. At the head of the latter was film-maker, advertising executive and national newspaper columnist (and now Chairman of the Australian Film Commission), Phillip Adams.

Adams launched a scathing attack on the violence of the film in the *Bulletin* magazine (1 May, 1979). He cited the 'dangerous pornography of death'.

Then after referring to George Miller's 'sheer brilliance' as a film-maker he observed that the film 'has all the moral uplift of *Mein Kampf*' and that 'movies like *Mad Max* must surely promote violence.'

Other critics, including myself, seemed less shocked and somewhat more enthusiastic about the film. In the Sydney *Sunday Telegraph,* Beverly Tivey described it as 'One of the finest achievements of the Australian film industry. The stunt work and special effects can stand with pride beside the best American productions.'

The late Geraldine Pascal, in the *Australian* said it was a 'clever, effective, futuristic horror fantasy – a sort of *grand guignol* of the consumer society.'

John Lapsely in the *Sun-Herald* called it a 'first-class horror movie' and 'a memorable experience'.

I wrote in the Sydney *Sun* that it was not blatantly violent: 'Much of the violence is implied rather than spread across the screen.' And: 'It is not going to be remembered as a great Australian film, rather as a very slick, professional piece of movie making.'

Whether *Mad Max I* will be remembered as a 'great' Australian film is clearly debatable and depends largely on taste. But it is undeniably a landmark film, not just for the Australian film industry and director George Miller and his partner, the late Byron Kennedy, but as a vehicle that would, ultimately, deliver Mel Gibson to certain international stardom.

It was not the only film that did it. But its success here in Australia, in Japan and Europe and, the US, following America's discovery of the sequel, *The Road Warrior,* gave Mel a unique, worldwide cult status.

Di Rolle, a publicist with Village Roadshow, the Australian distribution and exhibition chain that gambled on the first-time feature film director called George Miller and a futuristic road moved called *Mad Max,* remembers those first tentative days for Mel and Miller.

'I had been dealing with George Miller and the late Byron Kennedy, and they were still pretty raw in the business after making *Mad Max I,*' she recalled in Melbourne.

'Then they were trying to learn everything they could about the publicity side of it. Mel was there as their product, so to speak. Before our first meeting I expected him to be very good-looking, very in control and very confident.

'But when I first met him I was struck with how shy he was. He must be the shyest person I've ever met. Initially, he seemed to be totally uninterested in the whole publicity side of it. He didn't seem to me to have the star quality one would imagine, but he certainly grew into that.

'That first time he was terribly awkward and just interested in fooling around... a bit of a larrikin. He just wanted to get out with the boys.

'I don't think Mel will ever make a great interviewee, but that doesn't matter. So many great actors simply aren't the world's greatest orators.

'Robert DeNiro comes to mind. We attempted to interview him but he was extraordinarily inarticulate, yet he is one of the world's finest actors. John Travolta was very much the same, he was just lost for words. Really painfully shy'.

Di Rolle met Mel Gibson years later, when he was doing *Gallipoli.* 'I just couldn't believe the contrast that night when Mel came along. He was a different boy, very much the star. He looked a million dollars, and was very confident.

'He was just having a good time and enjoying all the trappings that stardom had won for him. And I thought, good luck to him! And he really is the most beautiful-looking boy. He has that special look of the Hollywood matinee idol.

'His eyes are beautiful and he had a lovely smile. I know he was born in America, but he has that lovely quality about Australian men, that turned-up smile and the larrikin element that's special to them. The rawness, a country outback sort of thing.'

TIM

M EL'S third film was shot entirely in Sydney, mostly
around the beautiful northern peninsula beach areas,
in the spring of 1978, for veteran Australian actor,
writer, director and producer Michael Pate.

Sydney-born Pate had worked in stage, radio and film productions (including *Forty Thousand Horsemen*) in Australia before
starting a very long and successful career in Hollywood, appear-
ing there in some thirty films. He also wrote a book *(The Film
Actor)* on his craft in 1970.

At this time he was by far the most experienced actor-director
working in the Australian industry.

The film was an adaptation of Colleen McCullough's first
novel *Tim* about a mentally handicapped young man's blossom-
ing relationship with a lonely spinter in her forties.

'I thought the book was basically a good idea, although I had
some reservations about it,' Michael Pate explained. He thought
the story was too delicate and too improbable but eventually
decided it was a kind of fairytale... a princess in a white tower
and a frog that becomes transformed.

Pate wrote the screenplay in the Queensland town of Bun-
daberg where he was making *The Mango Tree,* with his teenage
son Christopher in the lead. Chris recommended Mel for the
part. Mel's name had been mentioned by others, so Pate flew to
Adelaide to meet the young actor who was then working with
the State Theatre Company of South Australia.

He had not even signed the contract for the rights to the book
at the time; that happened only a matter of days before production started.

Pate had planned a somewhat different film from the one that
eventually found its way to the screen. He had originally planned
to have American actress Julie Harris in the lead. 'But Julie's son
was taken very suddenly ill and she felt she could not come out
to Australia,' Pate recalled.

Tim (Mel Gibson)

'So, within four weeks from the start, we had to choose another actress from the list offered to us by America, and we chose Piper Laurie.

'She seemed ideal, was in the right age bracket but it meant changing the whole script around. Instead of it being a more serious script, I made it a romance. As Piper was fair-haired, I was looking for someone dark. I saw a test that Mel had done for casting agent Mitch Mathews... he had a beard. It was just a head shot. He'd just done *Mad Max*.

'So I met him at the Festival Theatre in Adelaide, had coffee with him and then took him up to lunch with some friends of mine who owned a pub in North Adelaide. They're a very down-to-earth group of people, and of course he got on well with everybody.

Pate decided to cast him in the lead, and the shoot of *Tim* began. It wasn't all easy, as Pate recalled.

'Mel had to jump into the surf, and the water was bitterly cold. I could see him hit the waves, looking as though he was about to turn around and say, "Christ, that's tough!" But he did it, no complaints. And on the last shot, going down the beach, I suggested he run alongside Piper and then around her, like a puppy dog. He did a marvellous forward and backward run around her. It was just adorable the way they worked together.'

Indeed, Mel won the Best Actor award at the Australian Film Institute Awards in 1979, and Alwyn Kurts and Pat Evison won Best Supporting Actor and Actress awards as his parents.

A young Mel Gibson with Piper Laurie on the set of *Tim*

Mel Gibson and Deborah Kennedy in *'Tim'*

Scene from *'Tim'*

On the set in *Attack Force Z*

ATTACK FORCE Z

ATTACK *Force Z* is one of the two least known of Mel Gibson's films (along with *Summer City)*. His fourth film, it quickly followed *Tim*. It was packaged and produced by veteran Australian actor, director and producer John McCallum in conjunction with a company in Taipei.

American actor John Philip Law, best known for his role as the blind angel in *Barbarella*, was cast in the lead.

Mel was the second lead followed by Australian actor Chris Heywood and New Zealand-born actor Sam Neill, who had just made *My Brilliant Career* with Judy Davis.

It was a film initially beset by difficulties. Australian director Philip Noyce, who had made *Newsfront*, could not reach agreement with McCallum over a number of issues involving the style and content of the film.

Adrienne McKibbons, an Australian expert on Asian films who had done some research work for the production, had been there during pre-production. She remained on location after the changeover of directors.

'The film had a strange history. The original director, Philip Noyce, wanted to make an entirely different film from the one that the producer John McCallum and the eventual director Tim Burstall wanted. They wanted a shoot-'em-up film,' explained Adrienne.

'Philip left the production after only a matter of days in Taiwan and Tim was flown in to take over.

'Tim was, I think, pandering to John Philip Law at the expense of Mel, Chris Heywood and Sam Neill. Sam's character slowly disappeared; he wasn't nearly as important in the final result as he had been at the beginning.

'Mel had several run-ins with Burstall. I remember watching one where Burstall wanted to do something that seemed completely stupid and Mel just refused. Mel's character was supposed to be a crack commander, a special forces man who knew

41

what he was doing. Tim wanted Mel to rush in and find his gun was jammed and not know what to do. It just didn't gel, but it was so they could get a Kung Fu sequence with a Chinese actor who would then rush in and wipe out the Japanese with karate chops... which was totally illogical in the situation. The character, as he'd been built up, would never have rushed into the house without checking the gun in the first place to see whether it was jammed or not.'

According to Adrienne, Mel was quite rational about it all.

'I must say that while I was there I developed a lot of admiration for Mel and the way he approached everything,' she added.

'But in that incident, I remember, he was almost reduced to tears of frustration, which I thought was quite unusual.'

Despite the problem facing Burstall and his cast and crew, including long delays because of rain and the unfortunate upheaval involved in the changeover of directors, Burstall did a fair salvage job.

'Considering the chaos at the time, he did quite a job bringing the film together and gave it quite a visual quality,' Adrienne added.

The film was released briefly in 1980 but never found an audience. It has since found its way onto television and video. But it's not a film that Mel chooses to mention often among his list of credits.

Given the limitations of the script and the other difficulties surrounding the film, his performance was quite strong. Indeed, he made much more of his screen time than his better-known international co-star, Law.

GALLIPOLI

GALLIPOLI, Mel's fifth film, holds very mixed memories for the young actor. It was often a physically difficult film to shoot, with locations ranging from the desert and chilly night shoots on the South Australian coast to Egypt, where many of the cast and crew ended up with stomach complaints. At the end, Mel had a dose of glandular fever.

His opportunity for the role came indirectly through his professional concern to improve his craft on the stage, which had taken him after NIDA graduation for a very happy year to Adelaide. Through his time in theatre in Adelaide and his contacts there, the chance to appear in *Gallipoli* emerged.

The film would mean much to him personally and professionally, not only in Australia but internationally. He won his second Best Actor award – at the 1982 Australian Film Institute Awards – for his performance.

Mel first heard about plans to make a film about the Australian soldiers who went to Gallipoli three years before, while working with the South Australian State Theatre Company. Producer Pat Lovell suggested he look at the first draft of David Williamson's screenplay and the character of Frank. Director Peter Weir virtually hired him on the spot after a test and he met David Williamson soon afterwards.

Mel admitted at the time that he had no more knowledge about Gallipoli than any other person who had learned about it at school. He soon learned a great deal, not only by making the film, but because of detailed reading.

He found books by C. E. W. Bean, Australia's official historian of World War I, historian Bill Gammage's book and diaries and letters written by Anzacs. They were all so valuable that Mel adapted some of the material to his lines in the film.

At the time he also conceded that, like many young people, he hadn't given war much thought. It was history, but not recent

Off to war *(Gallipoli)*

enough to touch him. His feelings gradually changed as production of the film continued. He gained great respect for the men. Despite the poor conditions, he felt Australians were brilliant in battle, fearless and courageous.

The movie was shot on a number of diverse locations in South Australia, starting near the town of Beltana in the Flinders Ranges. Mel quickly built a strong rapport with his young co-star Mark Lee.

He felt Mark was a very unselfish actor and that Mark's character, Archie, was much more difficult to play than his own.

For a desert crossing sequence, the cast and crew moved to the edge of the dried-out Lake Torrens. It was a vast and primitive area, on the edge of the desert heartland of Australia, very harsh and very old. Mel was shocked when he discovered, after having stomped all over its grey surface, that it was covered with deadly funnelweb spiders. Dust storms and hot winds also made filming extremely difficult.

The most dramatic sequences of *Gallipoli*, of course, were the landing and battle scenes, shot on the rugged South Australian coast near the tuna fishing town of Port Lincoln which, for much of the Australian shoot, had been the film's headquarters. The coastal terrain was similar in many ways to the Mediterranean coast of Turkey, though steeper.

'It was an amazing visual recreation of the cove,' Mel recalled at the time.

Archie (Mark Lee) and Frank (Mel) ready for battle *(Gallipoli)*

The extras, mostly unemployed country men, also impressed Mel.

'They never complained. And we were very lucky. They were similar to the country guys from World War I; that's where most of the Australian soldiers came from.'

He remembered sitting in the specially dug trenches filming, with sand being whipped across the ground in his eyes. For a series of night shoots of the Gallipoli landing, Mel, his fellow cast members and extras sat for long hours in damp open boats off the beach with a persistent chill wind blowing up from the Antarctic.

He observed later, 'I watched these guys who were tough on the exterior but soft underneath. They were so much like the real guys, I have great regard for them. Every extra regarded his little role as very important, as the Anzacs regarded their roles, in a way.'

A comment by one of them stuck in his mind. 'Don't worry about the conditions, mate, we've got a warm bed to go home to... the Anzacs didn't!'

He said later, 'This spirit really affected me and these guys, whom I hope will become my friends. The spirit is still there. The years haven't stomped it out. And the extras were a major part in creating the mood for the film.'

The central character in this story of innocent and blindly courageous young men going off to a war they barely comprehended thousands of kilometres from home was Mark Lee's Archie. He was a bush kid, a champion athlete who became caught up in the national fervour of the time. It was a wonderful role and Mark did a very good and affecting job with it. But it was Mel who, ultimately, came across as the strongest character and through his part won further international attention.

This was partly because of his natural screen presence, but, more importantly, the character of Frank allowed Mel to use on screen some of that instinctive larrikin fun that is such a part of his personality. And, though he and Mark Lee were portraying youths, Mel brought to the role a certain maturity as well as his experience of having, by this time, done four films. It was by far his most mature performance and a landmark in his career.

Frank (Mel Gibson) and his mates impersonating British Officers. *(Gallipoli)*

MAD MAX II
(THE ROAD WARRIOR)

WITH the growing international success of the original *Mad Max*, it seemed inevitable that George Miller would make a sequel. But the former medical practitioner turned film maker had reached the point where, he said, he could not even look at the original.

Miller, a perfectionist as well as a stylist, had been somewhat frustrated by the technical and financial limitations that confronted him in the latter stages of that film. Problems with sound and the loss of the original editor to another film had limited what he hoped to do.

When the film finally became successful and Warner Bros asked about a sequel, Miller was cautiously keen. He had learned a lot about many aspects of the industry through producing and marketing *Mad Max*, but for a time he told friends and colleagues that he didn't care to tackle another like it.

'The first *Mad Max* was such a tough film to shoot, such a bitter experience, that there was no way in the world I ever thought I'd do another one,' he eventually admitted near the end of production on *The Road Warrior (Mad Max II)*.

Suddenly he found himself with a budget ten times the size of the original. 'George could now make the film he had really wanted to make with the first film,' Mel said just prior to the start of the shooting.

Gibson, who by now had done five films, including *Gallipoli*, was naturally important. Like Miller and producer Byron Kennedy, he had reservations about what they had achieved with the first *Mad Max* film.

Miller said at the end of the shoot: 'The core problem we had to confront in *Mad Max II* was how to retain the pace, the action and the emotional impact of the first film without just rehashing the story. One of the worst aspects of the industry is cynically made sequels.' Every care was taken to give the film a dimension beyond the original.

46

Mel Gibson as Max in *Road Warrior (Mad Max II)*

Crew members admitted that it was not until about five weeks into the twelve-week shoot that they realised what an enormous and spectacular undertaking the film was. Dean Semler, the cinematographer, was delighted with what he was getting. 'The stunts were the most spectacular I'd ever seen. And Mel was just great. An absolute professional, never late, and he knew exactly what was needed,' said Semler, who went on to shoot *Beyond Thunderdome*.

Mel's humour, in often highly uncomfortable circumstances of chilly, windy conditions, helped maintain a light mood.

'He was terrific with young Emil Minty, the lad who played the feral kid. They established a terrific relationship, with Mel gently taunting Emil. He has a really communicative way, particularly with young people,' one of the crew told me later.

Semler remembers, in particular, Mel's determination in doing one of the final helicopter scenes.

'The chopper had to come in with Mel lying prone and his head hanging outside the door. It was most uncomfortable. But I'll never forget the look on his face. Part of it was probably pain but the rest was acting. He was superb.'

The film's final two weeks had a grim list of injuries after more than two months of virtually trouble-free filming. Stunt co-ordinator Max Aspin recalls: 'I couldn't believe it. In a matter of a couple of days we had five people hurt.' Even a camel, frightened by the roar of a motor bike, lashed out and kicked one of the stunt men a good three metres, breaking one of his ankles. The hard work and agony paid off for one of the most thrilling chase sequences ever recorded on film.

The illogicality of the gangs of outlaw bikers having a seemingly inexhaustible supply of fuel for their gas-guzzling machines, when the entire premise of the story was based on the battle by a handful of people to protect the last remaining sources of fuel, was never explained, but few cared. The sheer energy and pace of the film caught the moviegoing public's imagination right around the world.

With Mel, once again the hero as the stoic, unflappable Max, delivering a solid presence on the screen, it became a worldwide hit. It also secured Mel's place as a box office name and a move star.

It was generally accepted, though never confirmed, that he could now command $1 million a film, the first Australian film star ever to do so.

Guy Hamilton, reporter (Mel), *Year of Living Dangerously*

Mel Gibson as Fletcher Christian in
Mutiny on the Bounty

Mutiny on the Bounty with Anthony
Hopkins as Bligh

Sigourney Weaver and Mel Gibson

THE YEAR OF LIVING DANGEROUSLY

PRODUCER Jim McElroy says he had no arguments with director Peter Weir's first and only choice for the lead in *The Year Of Living Dangerously*. After *Gallipoli*, which Weir had directed, it had to be Mel Gibson.

McElroy recalled, '*Dangerously* was in development when Peter got the offer from Stigwood and Murdoch to do *Gallipoli*, so he put *Dangerously* to one side. Gibson was in mind for *Dangerously* as soon as *Gallipoli* was being made. There were no problems getting him for the role, either, because the international aspects of his career didn't hit until after *Gallipoli* had been released. *Mad Max I* was out, but by the time he had become an international star we'd done the deal for *Dangerously*.'

McElroy had come to understand Mel's potential. 'He's got a magnetism, that magic indefinable quality that comes out of the eyes,' says McElroy.

'And in many ways I don't think that he's changed very much,' he adds.

'For a guy who's undergone all the pressures that he has and is, he is showing remarkable fortitude. And I think that's another reason he's a star.'

He remembers, for example, the enormous pressure he was under at the Cannes Film Festival in 1983 when he took a break in filming *The Bounty*, at that time in London, to join Peter Weir at the festival to help promote *The Year of Living Dangerously*.

'This guy was being besieged, and I mean besieged,' Jim, who was also representing the film as producer, remembered.

'There were funny little incidents like the sycophants who hang around and ingratiate themselves into the stars' lives, both male and female. Mel, like any other star, was a victim of that, but he was handling it extremely well. Sure, he's a hard liver, he likes having a good time. And I've enjoyed many a good night with him. Not for a few years now. But that shouldn't be misinterpreted... he just lives life to the full.

'You immediately feel close to the guy once you spend a little time with him. I remember in the first couple of days in Manila on *Dangerously,* we had bodyguards from day one for him and Sigourney. But Peter suggested that the bodyguards weren't necessary. The only trouble was the bodyguards wouldn't leave him. They decided to stick around with him... and they did. They were a couple of off-duty policemen. As it turned out, later on, we needed them.'

Mel played an Australian journalist in Djakarta during the reign and overthrow of President Soekarno in 1965.

It was by far the most sophisticated role Mel had ever played on stage or screen. The character of Guy Hamilton was several years older than the then twenty-six-year-old actor.

The film, adapted from Christopher Koch's novel of the same name, worked on various levels. It examined the political moods and conflicts in Indonesia at the time, Hamilton's dedication to his job and the ethical conflicts he faced upon learning secret information about communist aid. It also examined two relationships Hamilton had, one with his Chinese cameraman Billy Kwan (played brilliantly by New York actress Linda Hunt who, so deservedly, won an Oscar as best supporting actress) and a British consul employee, played in coolish style by Sigourney Weaver.

Mel told Paul Fischer later, 'It was complex getting to the character. I don't think that he's so complex. He's just very boring... it was a matter of making him interesting.'

A matter of going inside him? 'Yes, that's right. Well, I found out what it was like to be a journalist and what it was like to be a "green" journalist. I talked to a number of journalists and read their files. Really interesting. I wanted to find out what makes a guy do what Guy Hamilton did.
'Then there was the love story and his relation with the dwarf [Kwan] and him not knowing himself. And knowing that my face had to be in it, from the first to the last frame.

'That posed a few problems, because Hamilton never initiated anything. He is kind of the central figure, who makes this journey, the eyes of the audience; he goes through the east and meets all these interesting characters. He is really a reactor... or he reacts to all these things done to him.'

Mel did not meet his American female co-stars for *Dangerously* until he flew into Manila. 'We'd tied up Sigourney in Hollywood and of course Peter had found Linda Hunt in New York,' added McElroy.

'Mel immediately struck up a very friendly relationship with Linda Hunt, a New York stage actress who was to play Mel's cameraman Billy Kwan,' recalled Babette Smith, location publicist on *Dangerously*.

'It was very much a relationship of mutual trust. And the way the shoot was structured he had many more scenes with Linda up front in the filming. That was really nice to watch.

'Because Linda was really risking her neck in that role playing a man. And, so too, was Peter for casting her. But it was a very personal risk for her.

'Everyone, Mel, Peter, the entire crew, loved her from the moment we got to know her. And we all wanted her to succeed. Mel, in particular, was very supportive of her. One of the most interesting and perhaps difficult aspects for everyone was that once you knew her as Linda there was no way you could think of her as anything but a woman. That gives you some idea of how good her performance was.'

And while Mel and Sigourney Weaver worked together very well on the set, it was not until a rain sequence in which they both got drenched and ended up together in a car that the relationship really took off.

According to Babette, they simply had different approaches to their work.

'Mel had a more matter-of-fact, seemingly casual approach, *Year of Living Dangerously*

55

whereas the American style was evidently one of great thought processes and preparation, presumably born out of the method style of acting,' she added.

'Whatever was going on underneath the surface, Mel did not betray his thought processes to anyone. Sigourney, by comparison, seemed much more intense. It appeared to some of us on the set, at first, that they came from two different worlds. It just took a lot longer for the lines of communication between them to reach a relaxed and joking relationship. And, yes, the day most remember it happening was that rain sequence when they got drenched by the fire hoses in the street scene.

'There were all these huge fire trucks standing by and they had to get totally saturated. It did, literally, break the ice,' Babette added.

'The whole relationship from there on became much more relaxed.'

The sequence on screen, however, was nothing like the reality of the shooting, as Jim McElroy recalled.

For a start, the cafe and wharf sequences were shot in Metro Manila. The car sequence was actually shot on a chilly night at the Sydney showground some weeks later after death threats had forced the entire cast and crew to pull up stakes and return to Sydney.

'That sequence in the car where they begin to make love was actually set up in the car park at the showground. But, I tell you, it was so cold. It actually snowed that night in Chatswood, a northern Sydney suburb. It took us all night, and most of it was shot around midnight. The fires that you could see in the background were actually there to keep the crew warm.'

There was a real life sequel to the fiction of movie romance connected, indirectly, to *The Year of Living Dangerously*.

'It was an extraordinary incident during the Cannes Film Festival when we all went to dinner up in the hills behind Cannes,' Jim McElroy recalled.

'There was a table of about ten of us. This total stranger, a woman, I think she was French, just came over, grabbed Mel and stuck her tongue about six inches down his throat. Now, he hadn't requested it. It just came straight out of left field. That's the kind of thing he has to deal with.

'Mel completed the embrace with maximum decorum and minimum time and turned back to the table and started eating again... the woman went away. But there was nothing that Mel or anyone else could have done to stop what happened. It was all over so fast.'

Two-thirds of the way through the filming in Manila a series of death threats forced the crew and cast to quit and return to Sydney.

'The first thing we knew, a note was delivered to us,' Jim

McElroy recalled.

'It threatened our lives because it was felt the film crew's presence was imperialist and anti-Muslim. They wanted us to stop immediately. That was followed by a series of telephone calls to various individuals on the crew. I got one, Peter got one. Not Mel or Sigourney. They were anonymous, though mine was traced and the man was arrested. He had chosen a bad time to call... I was being interviewed by the police at the time. He was only a couple of blocks away. The calls turned out to be hoaxes.'

As news of the threats spread through the cast and crew, opinions varied about their seriousness. That division worsened as tension built up over the next three days. The reverberations of the threats had reached as far as the White House in Washington, eventually prompting the involvement of the CIA and a message from the Oval Office.

On top of all that MGM studios, the film's backers, were having serious thoughts about whether they should proceed with the film under the circumstances.

The key differences of opinion among the people on location in Manila were expressed by McElroy and director Peter Weir.

'I believed that there was no real threat, but that is irrelevant in the sense that it was a perceived threat from within the unit.

'And while that perception was around, filming could not continue. Peter ultimately took the decision to leave,' McElroy concedes.

'I didn't agree. My position was that there was no threat and if there was any particular threat, it could be contained. That was the advice I was getting from seven organisations including the CIA, the PIA [the Philippines Intelligence Agency], the Palace Guard Security, the police, the army and the Australian Ambassador to the Philippines. I expressed that view until the Sunday, during which time the security around the cast and crew had been stepped up dramatically and the decision was taken to leave. But we did continue to film on the Monday.'

The cast and crew had been informed about what was happening and, though each individual had his own opinion about the situation, everyone was calm and responsive to directions.

'By the time we'd got to Monday we were filming under very, very tight security,' says McElroy.

'Mel was great. He was perfectly calm and very co-operative and helpful. Of course, he had been aware of the situation concerning the death threats from the outset. We had the army and police and our own private security guards, and the area where we were filming was cordoned off. It would have taken a very heavy assault to be successful.

'It was a very tense time for both Peter and me, and I must say that I did support the decision to go. There was no flaming row as to whether we would stay or go. Peter eventually took the

With Peter Weir, director, and Oscar winner, Linda Hunt as Billy Kwan, on the set of the *Year of Living Dangerously*

attitude that he could not go on filming, that it was too unsafe. And that is a perfectly reasonable attitude for someone to take. But what I felt was vital for Peter, Mel, Sigourney and the rest of the cast and crew was to get filming again as quickly as possible, for two reasons. One, MGM were asking whether they wanted to continue making this picture. We were about halfway through and for MGM it was a question of: Do these guys know what they are doing? They weren't there, they were relying on reports. They'd made contact with the White House, and the White House was saying everything was fine.

'But where Peter and I did disagree was that I had to get shooting again. It was then late Sunday. I stated my intention to restart filming back in Sydney the following Saturday. We did have a disagreement about that. But Peter, I believe wisely, did agree with my logic on the thing and endorsed that. So we started again at 7 am on the Saturday. We had stopped shooting on Monday at midday so that seven principal cast members, including Mel and Sigourney, could catch a plane that night back to Australia. As it turned out, their passports didn't arrive at the airport in time and they missed the plane. That forced us, under the circumstances, to put them up, under assumed names, in a hotel near the airport. They left the following afternoon.

'We had tried to give the cast and crew the maximum amount of information possible. On the Monday we asked the principal artists and Peter to come to my suite and advised them as to what we were proposing to do. Mel was fine. Basically, Mel was happy to do just as he was asked. It was an extraordinary time. I got a crash course in security, some people were being alarmed, others were being cavalier.

'Amazingly, it had no evident effect on Mel. He was right back into the character when we restarted,' asked McElroy.

'But that is part of his being… he is so centred, this was just another part of the job of film acting. That shows what sort of guy he is.'

THE BOUNTY

SUPERMAN'S Christopher Reeve had originally been scheduled to play Fletcher Christian in a remake of *The Mutiny on the Bounty* for Italian producer Dino De Laurentiis and America's Orion Pictures. And, at that point, veteran British director David Lean had been involved in developing and planning the project for some six years.

When Lean and then Reeve withdrew from the project, a double Australian connection became involved with the film, (it was to be shot at Pinewood Studios in England and on a series of South Pacific locations including Tahiti and Gisborne, New Zealand). Firstly, expatriate director Roger Donaldson, who now makes his home in New Zealand, was brought onto the project. Donaldson had made a name for himself with two films, *Sleeping Dogs* and *Smash Palace,* both made in New Zealand. Then Mel Gibson was signed to play Fletcher Christian, the British naval officer who mutinied against Captain William Bligh, placed the captain and some loyal men in a rowboat and set sail in the *Bounty*. Clark Gable and Marlon Brando, two of the movie world's most powerful and charismatic leading men, had portrayed Christian on the screen.

When you looked around the cinema world in 1983, the number of leading men with the potential of playing Fletcher Christian could be counted on one hand, with a finger or two to spare. The role required an actor who could command instant respect on screen and yet had a rebellious and a romantic streak in him. Mel was almost perfect. Unfortunately, Robert Bolt's screenplay, based on the book *Captain Bligh and Mr Christian,* while it brought a new perspective to the high seas relationship between the proud and stubborn Bligh and the young but experienced seaman Christian, seemed to pay insufficient attention to Christian's character.

This left Mel in something of a quandary when it came to one

Mutiny on the Bounty

of the most dramatic and certainly the most crucial scene in the film... Christian's deckside declaration of mutiny and his confrontation with Bligh, played to powerful effect by Welsh actor Anthony Hopkins.

Mel told me later, 'I ended up having to virtually rewrite the scene myself the morning we were to shoot it. I had to, there was nothing in it when I got the script. I thought, What am I going to do here? The character was lacking and the only place to do something was in the mutiny scene when he flips out.

'I thought, the only way he can do it is by being like a loyal office boy, which is what he was, a public servant. He knew what job he had to do and got fed up with it one day. The only real threat he could make, as I saw it, was to knock himself off and leave them without a navigator. If they knocked Bligh off, then he'd threaten to kill himself.'

Having come to that conclusion, Mel unleashed a furious and emotional speech at Hopkins as the cameras rolled on the deck of the $4 million steel-and-wood replica of the original *Bounty*. Neither Hopkins nor Donaldson, or for that matter the crew, had any inkling of what Gibson had planned. Hopkins told me later, 'It was totally unpredictable. Mel just exploded and it caught everyone off guard. When Roger called "cut" the whole crew burst into applause.'

Mel admitted, 'You could tell by the look in Tony's eyes that he wasn't expecting it. A kind of "What are you doing, pal?" But it was in the nature of the Christian character. He went schizophrenic one day, whacko!'

Hopkins said he was deeply impressed by the then twenty-seven-year-old actor.

'We got on very well together. But I don't think Mel likes being a star. He told me he was scared at times, and that's good, because we're all scared. It helps the adrenalin. But he'll gain a lot more confidence with experience.'

THE RIVER

DESPITE Mel's hybrid American/Australian background, *The River* was his first truly American film. But in movie production terms, the American connection had started relatively early in his career. In only his third film, *Tim*, he had been cast opposite American actress Piper Laurie. American companies Warner Bros and MGM were involved in *Mad Max II* and *III* and *The Year of Living Dangerously*. And *The Bounty*, for De Laurentiis and Orion, though shot in England and the South Pacific with a British, Australian and New Zealand cast, was designated an American film for entry in the Cannes Film Festival.

But it was not unti late 1984 that Mel actually set foot in the US to work. He was cast by veteran director Mark Rydell in a quintessential American role, a battling farmer in Tennessee, coping not only with the vagaries of the elements but by a man, played by Scott Glenn, who has long fancied his faithful wife.

The film was also notable for one of the few bedroom sequences Mel has done in his eleven films to date, a tender but far from erotic or even passionate few moments with Sissy Spacek in a hotel room. The scene, though necessary at the time, seemed to have been underplayed by Rydell and the two stars. With a little more passion, it could have lifted the emotional level of the rest of the film. But Rydell, it appears, felt nice country folk reunited for the first time in weeks, alone in a bedroom, would be too restrained, or perhaps distracted by the dilemmas at hand, to enjoy each other.

Mel had to work with a voice coach to acquire an American accent, and an Southern accent at that.

It wasn't long before he was getting flattering, almost embarassing 'raves' from director Rydell. At one point, Rydell told the American press, 'I've directed a lot of great actors, Steve McQueen, Fonda, most of the big ones, but let me tell you, Mel is the most exciting. This guy is a cross between Steve McQueen and Montgomery Clift. If you watch him closely, there's an insolence and cheekiness there that few actors have. Look at those blue eyes and killer smile.' The remarks were widely reported.

When he returned to Australia in the middle of 1985, I asked Mel how he felt about such marvellous flattery.

'Oh, yeah, that Montgomery Clift stuff,' he said in typically self-effacing style.

'He never said it to me... I don't know what to make of it.'

The $20 million film was one of three that year to take a look at life in rural America. The others were *Places In The Heart* and *Country*.

The key seemed to be Mel's ability to take his time, to expand a moment on screen and allow us to see more effectively into the mind and heart of the character. It was something that was to be evident in *Mrs Soffel* under the direction of Australian Gill Armstrong.

The experience of making *The River* was mixed but essentially not difficult. There were some very uncomfortable scenes in floodwaters, but nothing too difficult compared with the *Mad Max* films or *The Bounty,* where thousands of litres of water in one sequence knocked Mel over and washed him to the end of the deck of the full-scale *Bounty* replica.

Of co-star Sissy Spacek, he told me when he returned to Australia, 'Sissy was... well, it just took a long time for me to figure her out, and I'm sure she took a long time to figure me out. But she was great, and I think you'll see that in the film.'

The film did not fare as well as perhaps it should have, critically or at the box office, but it provided Mel with another kind of film-making experience, working with a full American crew in the US, and in a character far removed from *Mad Max*.

He had taken his family with him; they rented a house in a small town nearby. Mel recalled the hospitality of the neighbours. 'They had no idea who Robyn and I were and they were just great, very friendly. The expression "Southern hospitality" is not a cliche and it's not phony. They're the most hospitable people I've ever come across, even baking cakes and bringing them.'

Mel was mildly amused at the reaction Robyn got when she took their three children out for walks or shopping. 'Robyn had dressed the kids in stripy tights and big jumpers, just the way she dresses them at home and local people laughed at them. They kinda looked a little different I guess.'

Mel remained with his family in America to make *Mrs Soffel* with fellow Australian director Gill Armstrong and cinematographer Russell Boyd.

MRS SOFFEL

AMERICAN actor Matthew Modine touched on the potential of a rarely used side of Mel's personality. Modine, who played Mel's brother in *Mrs Soffel,* was struck, like many before him, by the young actor's wonderful sense of humour, penchant for quick ad libs and often colourful jokes.

'I loved working with him. It was like we were really brothers. And Mel would try jokes, if they didn't work, he'd keep going until he got a laugh. I'm surprised that someone hasn't signed him to do a comedy. He's a very funny guy.' It's a comment that's been passed more than once in recent years.

But *Mrs Soffel,* hardly a comedy and shot in wintry Canadian locations, no doubt induced Mel to lighten the situations with his usual banter.

It was a film that allowed him to display his growing command of the medium, particularly in the key moments when the relationship between his character, Ed Biddle, and Mrs Soffel was being established.

Mrs Soffel, (Diane Keaton) was the wife of a jail warden where the Biddle brothers (Mel and Matthew), were serving a murder sentence.

Mrs Soffel's counselling of the inmates and her restless marriage leads gradually to an almost obsessive relationship which in turn has her freeing the pair and escaping with them.

Mel had to convince not only Mrs Soffel but audiences as well that he was worth her leaving her husband and children.

For it to work, their initially cautious, almost distant, exchanges through the bars had to kindle a gentle but sensual feeling.

While Diane Keaton's performance is a little too tentative, there are moments when Mel's is so deliciously flirtatious it fairly tingles with suppressed passion.

Mel said after the film that Diane had been a 'knockout' to

work with; clearly there was on-screen chemistry between them as the characters set out to escape to freedom, although, at first, their different backgrounds and styles in their craft seemed to make Mel a little wary.

By the end of the shoot they were good friends, delighting in various moments onscreen watching 'rushes'.

He was particularly delighted with director Gill Armstrong, later admitting that she had surprised him because he had not expected a great deal from her.

Gill said later she was delighted with his performance, describing it as very mature and adding that he was sexy, magnetic, sensitive and intelligent. Largely because of the subject and its 'downer' ending, *Mrs Soffel* did not do great business at the box office, despite mixed but generally good reviews.

Mad Max Beyond Thunderdome

'W'E'RE working in a new area with this one,' Mel said of the concept and script for *Mad Max Beyond Thunderdome.* 'Had this been just a remake of *The Road Warrior,* I wouldn't have done it. What would be the point? But this is a much more human story, even though it has that same kinetic energy.

'In *The Road Warrior,* Max was a sort of closet human being. In this one, his protective layers are peeled away. There's a lot more depth and humanity to the man.'

Once again, the success of the previous *Mad Max* film had opened the financial coffers, allowing director George Miller to fully use everything from script and production design to stunts and his casting. The budget had grown from around $400,000 for the original *Mad Max* to $4 million for *The Road Warrior* to $12 million, huge by Australian standards.

One of the characters, Aunty Entity, the chainmailed supremo of a place called Bartertown, had been written with an eye on rock singer Tina Turner. Miller was able to offer her the role, a chance she jumped at. So keen was she that she came to Australia some weeks before shooting to be involved with Miller and theatre director George Ogilvie in a series of workshops on the film.

Ogilvie's involvement was another Miller innovation. He ended up co-directing the film.

'It worked very well,' cinematographer Dean Semler recalled.

'They'd both be on the set, often standing behind the camera but more likely sitting at a table looking at a video split of the scene. George got the idea of using the video split from his time in America. It's not something I go for... I'd rather look through the lens, thank you, but it was obviously very worthwhile for a film of this magnitude.'

It was a unique combination that evolved between Miller and

Ogilvie more by chance than anything. Miller had involved Ogilvie on the Australian TV mini-series *The Dismissal* about the removal of the former Australian Prime Minister, Gough Whitlam, by proclamation of Governor-General Sir John Kerr in 1975. When one of the episode directors had to leave ahead of schedule, Ogilvie and Miller collaborated to direct the final scene. Ogilvie tended to devote his attention primarily to the acting, Miller to the set-ups and action.

Miller maintained a closed set on *Thunderdome* locations, largely under instructions from Warner Bros, who feared that cheap ripoffs would either pre-empt or follow the film, as they had done previous *Mad Max* films.

The film was shot in the rugged Blue Mountains, eighty kilometres west of Sydney, in a vast empty brickpit and ocean sand dunes, both in Sydney, and in the barren and remote gem mining area around Coober Pedy in South Australia.

Mad Max III – Max (Mel Gibson) with one of the wild children

For Mel, who had barely caught his breath after three films, it was a tiring exercise. But he barely faltered, despite sequences shot in conditions ranging from near-freezing water to temperatures of more than 40 degrees Celsius in Coober Pedy.

'He was quite incredible, and so was Tina for that matter. Five or six people collapsed in Coober Pedy from heat exhaustion and there was Mel in his black leather outfit doing scene after scene,' said George Miller.

The most spectacular sequence of the film, and arguably one that should have come near the end of the movie, was the Thunderdome battle, an ingenious confrontation between Mel and a chosen 'gladiator', suspended on heavy elastic bungey ropes and staged by stunt man Grant Page.

'Mel did all the sequences and apart from it becoming rather painful between the legs after awhile, he escaped unscathed,' explained Dean Semler, who did a superb job in both lighting and shooting the sequence.

Apart from some interviews with French and American magazines, Mel kept a relatively low profile during the shooting of the film. When it eventually opened in mid-1985 in the US, he toured there, but in Australia granted only one interview for a television program.

One of the most curious and disappointing aspects about the film's handling was the decision, apparently jointly by Warner Bros. and Kennedy-Miller, the production company, not to allow the film to be entered in the 1985 Australian Film Institute Awards. Though no direct reasons were ever provided publicly, it seemed the plan was to keep the film entirely under wraps for the American and Japanese buyers. Up to a point, this is understandable, but it robbed the many talented technicians, design and stunt people on the film of having their work recognised formally. Almost certainly, the film would have collected a swag of awards at the presentations.

For Mel, the performance was an expansion of Max's character in most ways and yet did not have the dimension of the first film. Once again there was no form of romantic encounter at all. Even the encounters with a stunning-looking Tina Turner were totally lacking in any sort of sexual friction. To many, including myself, it seemed a badly missed opportunity as Max went on his asexual way, perhaps never to return to the screen.

STAGE ACTOR

W HILE Mel's international career has been built on the success of the *Mad Max* trilogy, *Gallipoli* and *The Year of Living Dangerously,* his career at home in Australia has also covered television and, most notably, stage.

While television may provide access to a mass audience, it has been the least notable medium for him and the one that holds least interest. Despite appearances in five locally produced TV series and a telemovie, Australians would be hard pushed to remember any of his appearances. He appeared in the Crawford Productions police series *Cop Shop,* screened on the Seven Network in Australia, and their internationally successful family drama series *The Sullivans* (as a naval officer), screened by Kerry Packer's Nine Network.

He then appeared in three series for the Australian Broadcasting Corporation, the country's national broadcaster. They were *The Oracle, Tickled Pink* and *The Hero.* He followed that with the pilot telemovie for the Grundy Organisation's short-lived series *Punishment.*

But it has been in the 'live' theatre that Mel has not only sought to work fairly regularly (less so since his movie career took off), but been critically successful.

His professional stage career began after he graduated in 1977 from the National Institute of Dramatic Art, Sydney. In Adelaide, he took part in the chorus of Sophocles' *Oedipus* for the State Theatre Company of South Australia, where he was to appear in three other plays during 1978.

But then he was in the unusual situation of having already done two films, *Summer City,* for Phil Avalon, and of course *Mad Max I* in Melbourne. He was contracted to the State Theatre Company for four plays: *Oedipus,* Shakespeare's *Henry IV, The Les Darcy Show* and *Cedoona.* At this time, his name had been mentioned to actor and director Michael Pate, who

Mad Max under Thunderdome

Mad Max with a 'wild child'. *Mad Max III*

Mrs. Soffel. Kate (Diane Keaton), Ed (Mel Gibson) and Jack (Mathew Modine) Biddle after the escape

The Biddle Brothers *(Mrs. Soffel)*

70

Mrs. Soffel

Mrs. Soffel

cast Mel in the title role of *Tim* after recommendations by Mel's agents Bill Shanahan and Faith Martin. Pate flew to Adelaide, saw Mel perform and was impressed. After *Tim,* Mel was released from his SATC contract.

His next role brought him to national attention for his stage work. Australia's foremost stage actor and director John Bell cast him as Romeo opposite Australian actress Angela Punch's (now Punch-McGregor) Juliet for Sydney's Nimrod Theatre. The Nimrod had emerged as one of Australia's most adventurous theatrical entities.

Of Mel's performance, veteran *Sydney Morning Herald* critic H. G. Kippax commented on Saturday 24 March, 1979: 'This must be said for Mr Gibson – when his Romeo does grow up, after banishment, the effect is striking. His carriage sheds gaucherie, his voice deepens, he finds nobility.'

The public loved it, and it was taken by the company under Bell's direction, for a season at the Octagon Theatre, Perth.

Mel then did an Australian play *On Our Selection,* which has seasons at both the Jane Street Theatre and the Nimrod Theatre, Sydney. The part of Estragon in Beckett's *Waiting for Godot* followed.

Then came another commercial triumph, this time for the Sydney Theatre Company. It was the lead in *No Names, No Pack Drill,* an Australian play by Bob Herbert about a US marine during World War II who goes AWOL. Mel, with his American background, played the marine, nicknamed 'Rebel'. It was produced at the Drama Theatre in Sydney's spectacular Opera House and once again, Mel got strong reviews.

No Names has since been produced as a film under the title *Rebel,* starring another international heart-throb, Matt Dillon, opposite Australian singer, dancer and actress Debbie Byrne and Bryan Brown. Mel was offered the part of Rebel but was unavailable; he was doing *The River* and *Mrs Soffel* while *Rebel* was being filmed.

No Names was followed in his stage career by *Shorts,* produced by the King O'Malley Theatre and the Sydney Theatre Company, at the small Stables Theatre in Darlinghurst, East Sydney. Mel returned to the stage again in July 1982, after completing *The Year Of Living Dangerously.* This time it was opposite British stage and television star Warren Mitchell, who had won international fame in the British TV series *Till Death Us Do Part* (the inspiration for America's *All In The Family*). The play was Arthur Miller's *Death of A Salesman,* and Mel played Biff.

Mel's star had ascended internationally by this time. And, say people associated with the Seymour Centre where it was staged, it was the first time they can remember crowds of young fans hanging around the stage door for a glimpse, or better still, an autograph from him. The *Herald's* H. G. Kippax was most impressed with Mel's performance. On Monday 12 July 1982, he praised Mel and actress Judi Farr: 'Judi Farr and Mel Gibson as Willy's wife and son turn in superb performances.' And, later, referring to the emotion evoked in the play: 'Mr Gibson does it by uncovering, along with the shoddy, the real, rich devotion which is the mainspring of Willy's compulsions.' And still later: 'Mr Gibson gives us for about half the performance acting that is deceptively bland yet, with tensions lightly but insistently intimated, mysterious and uncomfortable.'

Mel's hectic film schedule through 1983 to the middle of 1985 and a much-deserved rest period after that, plus the development of a film project with producer Pat Lovell, has prevented him from returning to the stage. But it hasn't stopped him providing personal support for theatre generally and, specifically, for the Belvoir Street Theatre (formerly the Nimrod). When it faced eviction and closure, actors, directors and hundreds involved with the theatre rallied to raise money to buy the building in which the theatre had operated.

Mel had arrived back over the previous weekend in May 1984, after completing *Mrs Soffel* in Canada. Despite evident exhaustion, Mel turned out at a public meeting and media conference to lend his not inconsiderable voice of support. With a thick stubble covering the bottom half of that famous face, he told me at the meeting; 'We need the support of anyone who cares anything about the theatre and live entertainment to put money into the fund.' Mel became one of the 140-plus investors in the fund that eventually bought the building.

THE REAL MEL GIBSON

MEL'S private life has been and will continue to be as private as he can maintain it. Though he is far from a hermit and mixes easily with almost anyone on a day-to-day basis, he has learned to enjoy the relative solitude of his family life.

Long before he was a star of any standing, he never seemed to have too much trouble attracting girls, according to his friends. But he was only twenty-two when he met his wife, Robyn.

It happened in Adelaide, the city of churches, while Mel was with the South Australian Theatre Company on an initial six months' contract, his first professional theatre roles since graduating from NIDA. Robyn was a nurse and they met through her family connections at a boarding house where Mel had been staying. Her level-headedness, sense of fun and a certain stabilising effect attracted Mel. They were married less than two years later in a quiet ceremony at a Catholic church in Sydney's eastern suburbs, only a few kilometres from one of Mel's homes. The wedding, attended by the parents and relatives of both Mel and Robyn and some of his closest friends from the industry, was followed by a floating reception on Sydney's spectacular harbour. Again, it was very much a private affair; light food, drink and music, idyllic surroundings and privacy were just what Mel and Robyn wanted.

It's not too well known that Mel is now the father of four children. Hannah, his first child, was born when he was completing *Gallipoli* on location in Egypt. It was a traumatic time, but Mel had no choice but to share the birth of his daughter via the international telephone system. It was a highly emotional moment that, understandably, brought tears to his eyes and moved him deeply. Hannah is now six.

Three years later, Robyn gave birth to twin sons, Edward and Christian, no doubt a reminder of Mel's role in *The Bounty* at

the time. In 1984, their fourth child, another son, Will, was born.

As Mel comes from a family of eleven children, there is every likelihood the Gibson clan will grow further.

Mel's profound Roman Catholic upbringing is very much a part of his life ethic. He is still a staunch supporter of the Latin Mass, as is his father, but he realises and mostly accepts the changes that have occurred in the Church in the past two decades.

Life at home, according to those who know them, is very open and carefree with the children given priority in most cases. The Gibsons' Sydney home, in the beachside suburb of Coogee, is only a minute or so from one of the city's best beaches. Mel and Robyn, or sometimes just Mel, take the children for walks along the sand and into the rock pools at the end of the beach.

But even better is their farm in northern Victoria, set as it is in rich undulating countryside offering a wide expanse for the children to be themselves and grow up in an environment close to nature and far from smog and pressures of big cities and the special tensions that must surround one of the world's favourite movie stars.

In Mel's relatively short but hectically successful career one of the most interesting omissions has been the almost total lack of scandal that has surrounded his life, and it has not been for lack of living life to the fullest.

The most controversial headlines, if they could even be called that, dealt with a drink-driving charge in Canada during the shooting of *Mrs Soffel* and a minor encounter with the Australian Taxation Office. He laughs off the drink driving charge as an unfortunate incident and the tax issue was so trifling that it was passed off in the Australian press with just a few lines.

Linda Monmouth, a Sydney publicist, was looking after the launch of *The Year Of Living Dangerously,* including a hectic national capital city tour escorting Mel and his family. 'I remember going to pick Mel up at his home in Coogee and I was amazed at the lovely little old house that he lived in,' she recalled.

'It was in the process of being renovated and I only went as far as the hallway. There were all these kids' toys everywhere. Mel was pretty nervous but I guess I was more nervous, because he was very shy. I was nervous because of the Mel Gibson aura thing and when I realised that he was more nervous than I was, that made me feel a little bit more relaxed and we began chatting. 'I thought if you were able to put him and Robyn on a farm in gumboots with umpteen children, he'd be as happy as Larry!

'My single strongest impression of Robyn is that she is real, very real, in no way impressed by any of the Hollywood nonsense and prepared to stay in the background.

'I remember when *TV Week* wanted to do a pin-up of him, he

agreed to an interview, but flatly refused to do the pin-up. He just doesn't see himself as a pin-up.

An English magazine, *Woman,* wanted to do a story on the six sexiest men in the world. He totally resented that "sexiest man" thing. He said, "What does all that mean?" He said it all meant basically nothing; and all that sex symbol stuff was so much of a hype.

'Mel certainly has charisma, but personally I wouldn't put him up there with Robert Redford. He just doesn't have that effect on me.'

Dale Evans, an Australian television producer, first met Mel when she worked on the *Don Lane Show* in Melbourne in the early 1980s. 'He wasn't very well known at that time and I remember the producer saying, "Who's Mel Gibson? We'll put him at number three."'

'I'd heard so many stories about his humour at NIDA where, I believe, they used to call him "Kangaroo Feet", apparently from something he used to do in dance classes,' Dale recalled.

Her feelings about him reflect the kind of response Mel instils in most women both and off the screen.

'I actually met him for the first time when *Mad Max II* was released and he was sitting at the press conference … and I thought, "You poor creature!" He was just sitting there in this flood of camera flashes as if to say, "What do they all want to talk to me for?"'

'He's got vulnerability about him. You look at him and think, "I've just got to protect this person".' The Lane show's producers made sure they looked after their special guests. 'They had a very firm policy that everyone on the show be treated as a star, so it was always, "Mr so-and-so, we'll send a car for you and here's your dressing-room with the flowers in it". Mel got very embarrassed with that. He just didn't want to know. He said, "My name's Mel and I'll just sit on the steps and wait for the cab."'

'When he came back the second time (for *The Year Of Living Dangerously*) he'd had a great deal more exposure and a PR lady (Linda Monmouth) and Peter Weir were travelling with them as well.

'He was much more relaxed. I remember it was a Christmas show and I'd bought a lot of funny hats in Sydney; Mel and I were coming back on the plane to Melbourne. One of the hats was a giant copper Viking helmet with huge horns. Mel took it out of its wrapping and stuck it on his head. It was quite funny.'

Dale believes Mel's appeal is fairly obvious. 'The sexiest thing about him is his vulnerability and the fact that he is such a gentle person. I think he brings that out in people, too.'

Mel Gibson in the pilot television movie *Punishment*

Shelley Neller, a Sydney-based journalist specialising in the film industry, interviewed Mel twice, almost three years apart, in 1981 and 1984. She noted a significant change in him.

'By the second interview, he had realised that giving interviews was part and parcel of the price he had to be pay for success.'

She had gone to the first interview with certain fairly predictable preconceptions, drawn purely from his movie and media image.

'He looked like the strong silent type, fairly macho and not given to great verbosity, which turned out to be true,' Shelley explained.

'I'd been told he was like that and I'd seen him in *Mad Max*; it wasn't a Laurence Olivier role exactly, so I wasn't expecting an incessant flow of witty repartee. And I didn't get it.'

So, what sort of a man was she expecting?

'I think I probably expected him to be a bit more self-assertive, or maybe a bit more brittle than he was. In fact, he was very gentle, very quiet on both occasions. The first time, I think I was the seventh or eighth person to interview him, and they'd been pushing him pretty hard on *Mad Max II* during the day. I guess he was sick to death of talking about himself.

'He was fairly defensive, kept his head down and wouldn't even look at me ... I could hardly get any words out of him. And so I became low key in my manner. I became more gentle to see if he would respond to that, and he didn't really. It came down to my making statements about him and more or less asking him to agree or disagree.

'He was smoking and fidgeting, crossing and uncrossing his legs, drumming his fingers on the chair, looking around the room. I felt sorry for him because he looked very vulnerable, like a trapped bird who wanted to get out.'

Shelley, apart from her perceptive observations, is quite a fan of Mel Gibson, movie star.

'Oh, yes. I think he's very attractive,' she says with open enthusiasm.

'And I thought he was very attractive the second time I interviewed him, simply because he was much more communicative. I thought he was a very uncomplicated man who's called on to do all the verbal acrobatics that are part and parcel of being an actor and talking to the press.

'I just thought this was not one of his strong points ... he just wanted to act and get on with the job.

'The second time, the magazine I was writing for wanted all the stuff about his family, how he felt about his wife, what he did in his spare time and were his children important to him. That typical women's magazine kind of stuff.

'I knew that he loathed being interrogated about his family. Also, I'd been out of the country and hadn't been able to see the movie *Bounty* when I went to interview him.

'I was very low key. I told him that I felt nervous, which I was, and that seemed to shift the whole balance of the relationship. He sat right back in his chair and relaxed and looked at me as a human being rather than another interrogator. By this stage fewer people were getting through to him ... his agents were more selective about who was allowed to interview him.

'He was very relaxed. He'd been spending a lot of time with his family he said, having come back from that long bout of working, making *The Bounty*, *The River* and *Mrs Soffel* virtually back to back. Just hanging around quietly with his family seemed to have quite an effect on him. He wasn't smoking nervously, he wasn't twitching; he looked at me when he talked and he responded very generously and very openly, compared with the first time I saw him. His family is his mainstay, his security. I gather Robyn is very private and very quiet, and it seems to met that's very necessary because of the public demands of his career.

'Of course, he doesn't want to talk about his money. I said he was reputed to earn a million dollars a movie, and he passed it off with a laugh. I said, "Well?" and he said, "Oh, I don't want to talk about it." He was very nice about it.'

'On screen, he's beautiful. It's such a hackneyed word, but he has a very natural, assured sort of charisma. He knows absolutely who he is on the screen, whereas in private life you get the impression that if he does know who he is, he doesn't want anyone else to know. He's very guarded about himself.

'His attraction on the screen includes his voice. He has a wonderful speaking voice, and there is a paradox that you feel he's on the knife edge of danger. Maybe it's the roles, but they're the kinds of characters who create dangerous situations. You feel that at the flick of a switch, his personality could be aggressive and violent enough to deal with the danger on one hand and gentle and sensitive enough to deal with sensuality on the other.

'But I don't think he's the kind of person who's given to heavy analysis of his roles or of himself. He doesn't seem like the kind of person who makes his five-year grand plan for cinematic success. He gets on with his life.

'He's not given to bullshit, the way some people create an elaborate public persona. He's dedicated almost to disappearing off the page. But he's a sex symbol. Absolutely!'

American film publicist Paul Lindenschmid was present at a meeting between Mel and one of the great stars of the past five decades.

It began without Mel's knowledge in Los Angeles at the time of the rerelease of five of Alfred Hitchcock's classics, and

involved one of Hitchcock's favourite leading men, the inimitable James Stewart.

Lindenschmid, who is with Universal Studios, was handling the publicity schedule for Stewart, including visits to Europe and Australia. Later Lindenschmid handled the American release of two of Mel's films, *The Bounty* and *The River*. He has some cogent observations to make about Mel's stardom, compared with other major stars.

But first, Mel's connection with James Stewart.

'It was actually Jimmy who had asked about Mel. He said he'd enjoy meeting him, he really enjoyed Mel's work, and had a lot of respect for him. He liked the fact that Mel had done a lot of stage work and studied his craft. I must say that it certainly was not a disappointment when they met,' Paul recalled.

'Mel called us; I spoke to Mel's publicist before we left Los Angeles to come down to Australia. She had obviously called Mel and said that Mr Stewart would be in Sydney and would like the opportunity to meet. Mel called me straight away and we made arrangements that night to have dinner. Robyn came too.

'Mel and Jimmy got on very well. What you see of James Stewart on the screen is what you get, just a very understanding and kind man. They talked about films, mostly. Mel had mentioned that his favourite James Stewart film was *It's A Wonderful Life,* and he talked about Bogart, because Mr Stewart had worked with Bogey.'

The talk was not all about films. The conversation allowed the veteran star to offer a little advice. From an actor of Stewart's stature, what he said must have made an impression on the publicly shy actor who, in his relatively short career, has been professionally most co-operative when it has come to promoting his films.

'As I recall, Jimmy said it was important for Mel to keep his feet on the ground but to do publicity; it was really part of being a motion picture actor, and that it was important to promote films you were working on,' Paul recounted.

'Mel and Mr Stewart at that time didn't see each other again simply because Jimmy had such a heavy schedule, but they spoke on the phone. About six or seven months later Mel was in Los Angeles doing some work on *The River*. I know they planned to get together, but their schedules just didn't coincide.'

Paul's experience of handling two of Mel's films also provided a wider insight into the young actor's phenomenal rise. 'I handled *The River* and *The Bounty* for exhibition release in the United States; that is, I was handling the publicity after the films were made. Mel didn't tour for either of those films.'

Why has Mel developed such appeal? 'First of all, he simply has great screen presence and is very handsome and the camera really works with him very well,' Paul explained.

'Look, you know, I think it's just good, old-fashioned sex appeal! I think it's all in his eyes. And I've heard many, many people say that here.

'They asked Phyllis Diller what she would really like to do in life. She said she'd like to have breakfast in bed with Mel Gibson. His appeal in America is unlimited; he's very popular with all age categories.'

Inevitably, comparisons are always made. Paul paused for a moment when I asked him which American star of today he could compare to Mel.

'This might sound silly, but I'd say Robert Redford, because of his screen presence. And I've always thought of Mel being another Robert Taylor,' he added.

When Mel was doing *Bounty,* some of the publicity stills made him look like Robert Taylor. Both actors were really so striking … the black hair and the eyes. Mel is very similar to all those older stars. He has the good looks and the appeal that Gable had, that Robert Young had as a young man. We don't have too many of those around these days.'

But, I observed, Mel is not compared with current stars like Richard Gere and John Travolta. Why?

'No way! They're both good-looking guys, but you can't compare some of these young actors to the older ones who really had style, incredible good looks and appeal. Mel reminds me of a 1930s motion picture star.'

Paul Lindenschmid was also able to put into perspective Mel's current status in America in the light of his most recent films. By the time *The Bounty* and *The River* came out, America had seen *Mad Max I* and *II* and *Gallipoli.*

'Mel was an enormous star by then,' Paul said.

'He was by then in the top ten male and female stars in the US, maybe the top five. He had a key spot at the Academy Awards, a lot of articles on him and a lot of public interest. When he did *The River* I don't think any of that had diminished. Any change to Mel's status after that had nothing to do with Mel; if anything, it had to do with the film. To tell you the truth, I don't know why the story was done at all.

'Today, Mel is very big. People are awaiting his next film in anticipation and he is a very big box office draw. We all have our crests; you have a winning film and you're on top, then you have a couple of films that don't work and you're a little lower. Instead of number one, you're number five. Put Mel in a good film and he's right at the top again. But *Mad Max* is not the kind of movie that enhances the sex symbol image. Mel needs something with meat in it.'

Paul's own choice of his favourite Mel Gibson film may come as a surprise, but when you reconsider the role and his performance it's not so strange at all.

'My favourite film was *Tim*. For Mel I think the film worked very well because it showed what his abilities as an actor and a performer really were. He didn't have to say much. If you were deaf and couldn't hear a word, you knew exactly what was going on. I loved the music. It showed that Mel can get in front of a camera and not say much and yet get across an enormous amount.'

What does the future hold for Mel Gibson in the movie world? It is limited only by his own ambitions, the scripts he is given and the decisions he and his agents make. His rise to international stardom has been relatively rapid, though by no means unique.

Personally and privately, he is a very level-headed young man. His openness and trust of people has at times seemed mildly detrimental to him when his casual remarks have been quoted by a voracious press ready to regurgitate anything about their latest target. He has rarely complained but, it seems, he has learned to be a little more tactful. It has certainly not damaged his career and, as he matures both as a man and in his craft, it's hard to find anyone who doesn't believe his best work is ahead of him. He is not about to be steamrollered into anything.

His family and their lifestyle is of prime importance to him. Early in 1985 he purchased a small farm in northern Victoria, several hundred kilometres from either Sydney or Melbourne. The nearest town is a hamlet that has taken Mel, his family and their desire for privacy to heart. Locals decline to talk about him, other than to acknowledge that he comes into town, does the shopping and enjoys a beer at the local hotel.

There is a constant stream of scripts sent to him from around the world, filtered through his Australian agent Bill Shanahan, but Mel is also involved in projects of his own. One of his next films will almost certainly be *Clean Straw For Nothing,* based on a novel by the late Australian author George Johnston, and set in Greece and Australia. It is being developed in association with producer and close friend Pat Lovell, whom Mel first met prior to making *Gallipoli.* Then again, Mel could decide to retire from the screen, prematurely, if not forever at least for a reasonable time, perhaps to relax and farm, maybe to concentrate on stage work for a while.

Whatever he chooses, though, he has carved his own niche in film history in less than ten years, not just for personifying on screen the now legendary Mad Max. His characterisations in *Tim, Gallipoli, The Year Of Living Dangerously* and, to a lesser degree, *The River* and *Mrs Soffel* will be remembered and enjoyed by movie fans for a long time. Like his millions of fans, I look forward to seeing what kind of cinematic surprises he has in store for us.

CREDITS

FILMS

Summer City (1976)
Director: Christopher Fraser, screenplay Phil Avalon. Production company: Avalon Films, Sydney. Cast: John Jarratt, Mel Gibson, Phil Avalon, Steve Bisley, James Elliott, Debbie Forman.

Basically a road movie, set in the rock and roll era of the early 1960s. Four friends, Robbie, Scollop (Mel Gibson), Boo and Sandy, head north out of Sydney for a wild surfing weekend. They camp on a beach near a small town and Boo (Steve Bisley) seduces a local virgin (Debbie Forman). The following day, her father, a somewhat crazy war veteran, comes after them armed with a gun, leading to a bloody and violent ending.

Mad Max (1977)
Director: George Miller, screenplay James McCausland and George Miller. Production company: Mad Max Pty Ltd (later Kennedy-Miller Productions). Cast: Mel Gibson, Joanne Samuel, Hugh Keays-Byrne, Steve Bisley, Tim Burns, Roger Ward, Vince Gil.

Described simply and effectively as a 'gothic horror story set in the near future'. The inter-city highways have become white line nightmares, an arena for a strange apocalyptic death game between nomad bikers and a handful of young cops in hotted-up pursuit cars. Max Rockatansky (Mel Gibson) a highway patrol cop, is responsible for the death of a crazed biker. When Max returns to his woman she tries to persuade him to quit, but Max doesn't want to talk about it. When he returns to the main force patrol head-quarters, he is presented with a supercharged pursuit car as an inducement to continue. A gang of nomad bikers come to a small town nearby to collect the remains of the crazed biker and violence erupts. When one of the gang is set free on a technicality, Max and his colleagues are given an open ticket to clean up the roads. One of Max's closest friends dies in an act of revenge by the bikers. Horrified, Max quits the force and heads across country with his wife,

Jessie, and child. After a series of confrontations Jessie is badly hurt and their child killed. Slowly, the madness grows in Max's eyes, he rejoins the force and one by one hunts down the bikers.

Tim (1978)

Director: Michael Pate, screenplay Michael Pate (adapted from Colleen McCullough's novel). Production company: Pisces Productions, Sydney. Cast: Mel Gibson, Piper Laurie, Alwyn Kurts, Pat Evison, Peter Gwynne, Deborah Kennedy.

Mary Horton (Piper Laurie) is a single woman in her mid-forties. She works as a personal assistant to a city businessman. She is well off, if a little lonely. One day a handsome young man, Tim (Mel Gibson) comes to do some odd jobs at the house next door. Mary hires him, gradually befriends him and discovers that he is slightly mentally retarded. A warm, friendly relationship evolves between Mary and Tim, as she comes to enjoy the childlike trust he places in her. At home, however, Tim's life undergoes several changes, one of them traumatic. His sister marries and his mother (Pat Evison) dies. It becomes evident that Tim's affections are now all directed to Mary. She consults an expert about the relationship, acknowledging as she does so, that her feelings for him run deeper than simply friendship. On his advice, Mary marries Tim.

Attack Force Z (1978)

Director: Tim Burstall, screenplay Michael Cove. Production company: John McCallum Productions, Sydney-Central Motion Picture Corporation, Taipei. Cast: John Phillip Law, Sylvia Chang, Sam Neill, Mel Gibson, Chris Heywood, John Waters.

An action adventure film set in Asia during World War II and based on the exploits of Australian soldiers in the special Z Force teams used as guerilla units against the Japanese. Mel plays Captain Paul Kelly. The unit's destination is an island off the coast of mainland China; a Japanese scientist has been shot down. It's believed that he holds the key to ending World War II. A special attack force is sent in to get him off the island and take him back to the Allied forces. Their mission is aided by a Chinese man and his daughter and young son. But as the mission proceeds there is conflict between members of the mission as their plans start to go awry.

Gallipoli (1980)

Director: Peter Weir, screenplay David Williamson. Production company: Associated R. and R. Films, Sydney. Cast: Mel Gibson, Mark Lee, Bill Hunter, Robert Grubb, David Argue, Bill Kerr.

Two Australian boys, one from a farm, the other a railroad worker, enlist in the Australian forces to fight in Europe in World War I. They are, like so many other young men at the time, idealists, innocents, with only the propaganda published in newspapers and the mixed feelings of their families to guide them. Archie (Mark Lee), more than Frank (Mel Gibson), is the wide-eyed innocent as they befriend other young soldiers, plucked from shops and farms to fight a war they can barely comprehend in a land that is almost totally alien to them. They arrive in Egypt and briefly and boyishly enjoy the exotic delights of the markets, the women and the pyramids before being plunged into the bloody reality of war on the cliffs of Gallipoli in Turkey. Their friendship and that of their mates counts for little as, wave by wave, they charge blindly into the gunfire of the enemy.

The Road Warrior (Mad Max II) (1981)
Director George Miller, screenplay George Miller and Terry Hayes with Brian Hannant. Production company: Kennedy-Miller Productions, Sydney. Cast: Mel Gibson, Bruce Spence, Mike Preston, Vernon Wells, Emil Minty, Virginia Hey.

In a barren, lawless land urban society has been destroyed by the effects of a war which blazed across the oilfields of the Middle East. Fuel is now the only currency of value, the most precious commodity in the world. Gangs of outlaw bikers and packs of mechanised marauders roam the countryside seeking what few litres of gas they can lay their hands on. A small band of people man a desert 'fortress' and series of humpies that protect the bikers when into their midst stumbles a battle-worn warrior, a former police pursuit cop, Max Rockatansky (Mel Gibson). Max is having a hard enough time surviving in his own right, let alone taking on the marauding hordes. But, persuaded by the desert people, Max agrees to help them, leading a spectacularly heroic escape in a juggernaut.

The Year of Living Dangerously (1982)
Director Peter Weir, screenplay David Williamson, Peter Weir, C. J. Koch, adapted from the novel of the same name by C. J. Koch. Production company: McElroy and McElroy. Cast: Mel Gibson, Sigourney Weaver, Linda Hunt.

Guy Hamilton is an ambitious Australian television reporter in Jakarta on his first overseas posting in 1965. He is befriended by Billy Kwan, a Chinese-Australian news cameraman who is a dwarf. The regime of Indonesia's charismatic dictator, President Soekarno, is on the brink of political turmoil. Through his friendship with Billy, Guy not only gains inside information about a possible rebellion but an understanding of both the Indonesian people and what Soekarno represents. Billy also introduces Guy to an attractive British Embassy attache, Jilly Bryant. An often fiery romance, heightenend by the uncertainties of what is happening around them, grows steadily against the backdrop of mounting local tensions and violence. Adding to the emotional complexity is the haunting effect of their common friendship with Billy. When Billy dies dramatically, Guy finds himself struggling for his own life and a chance for freedom.

The Bounty (1983)
Director: Roger Donaldson, screenplay Robert Bolt. Production company: Dino De Laurentiis. Cast: Mel Gibson, Anthony Hopkins, Edward Fox, Laurence Olivier, Daniel Day-Lewis, Bernard Hill, Wi Kuki Kaa, Tevaite Vernette.

An Admiralty court-martial hearing presided over by Admiral Hood listens to the story of a mutiny by men and officers on His Majesty's armed vessel the *Bounty*. The story is recounted by Lieutenant William Bligh who, with a handful of loyal men, has miraculously sailed an open boat about 6400 kilometres before finding land after a mutiny led by Fletcher Christian. Bligh has been commissioned to go to Tahiti to recover 1000 breadfruit plants and take them to the West Indies for replanting, to counter the food embargo placed on England due to the American revolution. He invites his friend, the young but experienced sailor Fletcher Christian, to join him as his third-in-command and as a navigator. By the time their voyage on the *Bounty* takes them into the storms off Cape Horn, the men have become restless. When Bligh persists in heading on in what the men consider suicidal conditions the situation almost reaches mutiny. Christian, amid great hostility, is elevated to second-in-command. They finally arrive in Tahiti where the simple, idyllic lifestyle, the access to the beautiful island women and the built-up resentment against Bligh and Christian begin to take their toll. A number of the men refuse to leave and even Christian is loath to respond to Bligh's commands. Grudgingly, the men reboard to continue their journey, but under the obsessive, rigid and sometimes ill-judged discipline of Bligh the situation eventually reaches an explosive climax. Christian, shattered and disillusioned, confronts Bligh on the deck and organises the mutiny, putting the disbelieving and enraged Bligh and his supporters into an open boat, literally adrift to find their own destiny.

The River (1984)
Director Mark Rydell, screenplay Robert Dillon and Julian Barry. Production company: Universal Studios. Cast: Mel Gibson, Sissy Spacek, Scott Glenn. Farmer Tom Garvey (Mel Gibson) needs the resources of the river that flows through his land and the rain that keeps it flowing, but too much of a good thing will destroy him. When the river floods it tears the heart out of his land. Tom and his family battle to hold back another raging torrent to save their crops, their few head of stock and farmhouse. Even substantial success still leaves him with such damage that he needs more money. But this time, the bank is not prepared to accommodate him. But the fate of the weather and

benevolence of the local manager are not the only things that hang threateningly over Tom's future. A former suitor of his wife's is looking to buy up the rest of the land and turn the valley into a huge dam. Tom, desperate for money, seeks 'scab' work in a nearby city's iron foundry. With his wife caring for the farm, their separation strengthens his resolve and their relationship. But when he returns eventually, he is faced with a double blow. The river is in flood and forces have been marshalled to finally break Tom's resolve and take away everything he has fought for.

Mrs Soffel (1984)

Director: Gillian Armstrong, screenplay Ron Nyswaner. Production company: Metro-Goldwyn-Mayer. Cast: Diane Keaton, Mel Gibson, Matthew Modine, Edward Herrman, Trini Alvarado, Jennie Dundas.

In the summer of 1901, Ed and Jack Biddle, two small-time criminals, are sentenced to hang for the murder of a grocer killed during a burglary they committed on the outskirts of Pittsburgh. A relatively obscure person assists their escape; Mrs Kate Soffel, the wife of the prison warden. She has maintained her Christian routine of delivering Bibles and words of comfort to the various prisoners and is at first intrigued, then gradually infatuated by the magnetic personality of Ed Biddle (Mel Gibson). Through his mixture of regret, cheekiness and humility and her beguiling, uncertain response grows a passion so powerful that it will engulf both their lives, provoking Kate to help Ed and Jack escape into the snowbound countryside and a bid for freedom. Once free, however, Ed cannot let go of the woman who has saved him.

Mad Max Beyond Thunderdome (1985)

Directors: George Miller and George Ogilvie, screenplay George Miller, Terry Hayes. Production company: Kennedy-Miller Productions. Cast: Mel Gibson, Tina Turner, Bruce Spence, Helen Buday, Frank Thring, Angelo Rossito, Angry Anderson, Robert Grubb.

A new society has risen from the ashes of a civilisation destroyed, a throwback to man's private past where basic technologies from bygone ages are employed for survival in a market city called Bartertown. Anything, everything is traded; a sip of water, a human life. At the centre of Bartertown is Thunderdome, a circus of justice where differences are settled and the public entertained. The code of Thunderdome is simple: two men enter, one man leaves. Max Rockatansky (Mel Gibson) a nomadic warrior, arrives out of the wilderness in search of his stolen camel train. Before he can recover his belongings, he finds himself confronting Aunty Entity, Bartertown's feudal founder. She has a deal for him: he must face the Master Blaster, who aims to control Bartertown, in the Thunderdome. Suspended from elastic bungey ropes Max takes on Master Blaster, a massive, helmeted giant and his 'brains', a clever dwarf who controls the Underworld where methane gas is converted to the power that runs the town. Their confrontation is bizarre, swinging and bouncing up and down and from one side of the circular arena as they grasp for strategically placed weapons. This is a fight to the death. Max gains the upper hand but shows leniency. He is banished to the desert and is eventually found and saved by a tribe of wild children who live in an oasis called the Crack in the Earth. They are descended from survivors of a plane crash who await the return of Captain Walker, their saviour. Max is hailed as the long lost aviator who will lead them to Tomorrow-morrow-land. Inspired but confused, Max leads the fifty children back to Bartertown, where they steal a huge old locomotive train used for the gas conversion and are chased by Aunty Entity's men.

THEATRE

Graduated from the National Institute of Dramatic Art in 1977.
Oedipus (1978) State Theatre Company of South Australia, in the chorus
Henry IV (1978) State Theatre Company of South Australia, played Godshill/Vernon/Mouldy/Mortimer
The Les Darcy Show (1978) State Theatre Company of South Australia, played Father Coady
Cedoona (1978) State Theatre Company of South Australia, played Chuck
Romeo and Juliet (1979) Nimrod Theatre at the Seymour Centre, Sydney and Octagon Theatre Perth, played Romeo
On Our Selection (1979) Nimrod and Jane Street Theatres, played Sandy
Waiting For Godot (1979) Jane Street Theatre, played Estragon
No Names, No Pack Drill (1980) Sydney Theatre Company at the Sydney Opera House, played Rebel
Shorts (1981) King O'Malley Theatre and Sydney Theatre Company at the Stables Theatre
Death of A Salesman (1982) Nimrod Theatre Company at the Seymour Centre, played Biff

TELEVISION

Cop Shop (Crawford Productions), *The Sullivans* (Crawford Productions), *The Oracle* (Australian Broadcasting Corporation), *Tickled Pink* (ABC), *The Hero* (ABC), *Punishment* (Grundy Organisation).